Conspiracy: Book II

In Pursuit of Justice

Cover design by Kent Grey-Hesselbein,

KGB Design Studio

Manchester, TN, USA

http://kghdesign.nvaazion.com/

Reviews of Conspiracy in the Town That Time Forgot:

I'm not usually one to read very much, but when I got this book on a Friday afternoon, I took it home and started reading it that evening. I finished it the next morning. A really great book! I could hardly put it down!

Jim Fuller, Channel 6 TV, Tullahoma, TN.

5.0 out of 5 Stars—Savvy Sheriff Saves the Day Author St. Clair paints an endearing portrait of savvy small-town Sheriff Ron Cunningham without a hint of irony. Much of the dialogue seems to be lifted straight from audio surveillance, giving a real-time feeling that keeps the reader on the edge of his or her seat. Juxtaposing humorous vignettes (i.e. Ron's creative campaign against indecent exposure) against the high suspense and drama surrounding the contract on the good Sheriff's life, St. Clair makes this true story immortal.

Emily O. Roberts, Asst. District Attorney, Coffee County, Tennessee

This book is great! You have a best seller!

Bobby Carter, attorney at law, Tullahoma, TN

This is a truly great work! I highly recommend it to all.

Nate Wolf, insurance executive, Kansas City, Kansas

5.0 out of 5 stars—A Most Shocking Read. This drama is powerful and thought-provoking. With a contract out on his life, it was quite shocking to read the actual descriptors related to the countless times that Ron, a small time sheriff in the state of Tennessee, managed to escape with his life intact. Even in situations whereby he was absolutely terrified, which you will shudder at knowing, he was down right adamant that justice would prevail. Willing to put his life on the line, I simply had to keep reading. In truth, it is my belief that a higher power intervened so that he could tell his story, courtesy of Stan. As a result of this book, their first collaboration, Stan St.Clair and

Ron Cunningham have proven that they are a remarkable team.

Editor Michele Doucette, author and teacher, Newfoundland, Canada

Editorial Review of this book:

Over the years, Ron Cunningham has endured numerous personal attacks in his role as a law enforcement officer. Always one to stay true to his personal beliefs, he has had to face a multitude of challenges. Shannon, Leah and Yolanda all share some pertinent childhood memories about the time when their father was the Sheriff in Lynchburg, Tennessee. As a reader, I found that this made for fascinating reading, adding important detail to the overall story. As Ron himself alludes to in his personal introduction, *fasten your seat belt and hold on* as you take a ride back into the past; a past that will leave amazed at how the events played out, given his bravery and fortitude.

Michele Doucette, editor and author of A Travel in Time to Grand Pré

Conspiracy:

Book II

In Pursuit of Justice

by

**Ron Cunningham
and
Stan St. Clair
with Linda Hudson Cunningham**

Contributions by

Shannon Cunningham Trzcinski

Leah Cunningham Hulvey

and Yolanda Cunningham Clark

Edited by Michele Doucette

© 2010 by Ron Cunningham and Stan St. Clair

St. Clair Publications

All rights reserved. No part of this publication may be reproduced or transmitted in any form by any means electronic or mechanical, including telecopy, recording, or any information storage and retrieval system now known or invented, without permission in writing from the publisher, except by a reviewer who wishes to quote brief passages in connection with a review written for inclusion in a magazine, newspaper or broadcast.

ISBN 978-0-9826302-6-6

Printed in the United States of America by

St. Clair Publications

P. O. Box 726

Mc Minnville, TN 37111-0726

http://stan.stclair.net

Conspiracy: Book II - In Pursuit of Justice

TABLE OF CONTENTS

Ron with first Conspiracy book	12
Dedication	13
Special Remembrances	14
Acknowledgements	16
Our Memories "Daddy's Girls"	18
Shannon	20
Leah	36
Yolanda	45
Co-author's Notes	57
Ron's Introduction	61
Chapter One	63
Picture—Lacy "Moon" Brown	67
Chapter Two	68
Chapter Three	74
Chapter Four	79

Conspiracy: Book II - In Pursuit of Justice

Chapter Five	82
Picture — Ron back in Lynchburg	87
Chapter Six	88
Chapter Seven	92
Chapter Eight	101
Chapter Nine	109
Chapter Ten	114
Picture — Redd's Grocery crew	124
Chapter Eleven	125
Chapter Twelve	135
Chapter Thirteen	141
Picture — Miss Mary Bobo's	149
Chapter Fourteen	150
Chapter Fifteen	157
Picture — Larry Wallace	167
Chapter Sixteen	168
Picture — The two-seater at Moon's	179

Chapter Seventeen	180
Chapter Eighteen	185
Chapter Nineteen	194
Epilogue	201
Pictorial	209
Joseph Colonel Cunningham	222
Bibliography	232

Ron with the first book

(From *Tullahoma News*, used by permission)

DEDICATION

Dedicated to all law enforcement officers across the country. I'm sure all of you have experiences you could share. This is mine.

The constant struggle to balance your historical experiences and achieve more than seems possible, sometimes is a thankless job.

Thanks for your commitment and all you do for your community, state, and country.

Ron Cunningham

SPECIAL REMEMBRANCES AND RECOGNITIONS

Former Coffee County, Tennessee Chief Deputy and Franklin County Sheriff Department Investigator Charles Jerry Crabtree; killed in auto accident near Winchester, Tennessee on January 29, 2010, while on duty.

Spring Hill, Tennessee Corporal Jeremy McLaren, killed in auto accident Sunday, February 7, 2010, while on duty in Maury County.

Tullahoma, Tennessee Corporal Kerry Hayworth, passed away October 7, 2008.

We wish to express our sincere appreciation to each of these fine officers, and our best wishes always to their families. May their service never be forgotten.

ACKNOWLEDGMENTS

It is a blessing and tribute to know that God is the one and only sovereign power and He watches over us all.

Bow low before God, stand tall before men, and to know victory is to know your enemy.

I would like to thank the many people who helped me make this book possible. To my beautiful wife, Linda, a special thanks for encouragement, sound advice, good teaching, great company and lots of good ideas. A special thanks to "Daddy's girls", Shannon, Leah and Yolanda. I would have been lost without them.

The stories in my head would never have been translated to words on paper were it not for the writer, Stan St. Clair. Thanks Stan.

I am grateful to my investigative staff and friends within the Law Enforcement community. They have been gracious enough to share insight and vulnerability.

A special thanks to Assistant District Attorney General Emily Roberts who graciously agreed to review and summarize court records, and to other lawyers and friends who have read the first book and given reviews.

Note: there are many people who helped to make this book possible. If anyone does not find his or her name here, please know that its absence was an oversight, and your contribution is deeply appreciated.

Ron Cunningham

OUR MEMORIES

"DADDY'S GIRLS"

In their own words

Ron and I both felt that the following childhood memoirs of his three dedicated daughters were so distinctive and added so much depth to the saga of this era in Moore County history that they deserved to be placed in the beginning to be devoured first by every reader.

Each girl was asked by Ron to independently recall their most indelible memories from that long-bygone fragment of their lives. Though somewhat overlapping, these synoptic accounts serve together to mirror these bittersweet days in an unforgettable manner.

My sincere thanks to each of these special

ladies for a job well done.

Stan St. Clair

Shannon

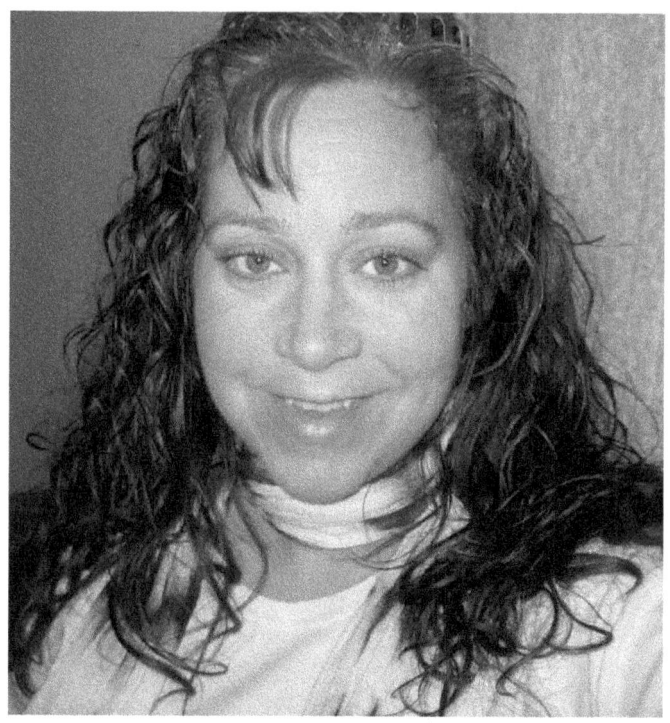

Growing up the daughter of the sheriff gave experiences with rich memories not usually afforded in one's childhood. I, Shannon, consider myself very blessed. In the small town of Lynchburg, everybody knows everyone, especially when your dad was the sheriff.

However, I never felt frustrated by that fact, because to me, everyone felt like family.

Family. I love my family. My dad is my hero. My mom was always there taking care of us. My sisters, well, no one could love them more. I am the oldest and was always watching out for them. There are only thirteen months difference between Leah and me. So, we did everything together. Yolanda is a couple of years younger, so she usually watched us do everything together.

We lived in the jail. I love people's reaction when they hear me say that. What seems crazy and strange to them was everyday, normal life for me. I thought nothing of it. I was five years old when we moved in there. We lived there for several years. As a child, it seemed so big to me. The jail was on the corner of the square. As with most very small towns, everything closed at five o'clock. That's when magic would happen, especially on those long summer nights! The local townsfolk would go home, the tourists headed back to their hotels, and the square would become our playground. My sisters and I felt like we owned the place! We loved having it all to ourselves. One of my favorite memories was when my sister, Leah, and I would get a pair of handcuffs, cuff our ankles together, and take off having a three-legged race.

I learned to ride my bike on those sidewalks, around and around I would go. Leah and I loved to ride, and Yolanda would try to keep up on her tricycle. I remember doubling on my bike once with a friend. We decided to ride behind the jail where, at the time, was a bunch of loose gravel. All of a sudden, my friend hit the brakes, and I went flying through the handle bars. I hit the loose gravel and slid for a long time, finally stopping just shy of a big puddle. My friend helped me up. I was a mess. My knees were split open. My arms, knees and my lower lip had gravel and dirt embedded in them. I hobbled up to the jail. When we got there, I knew it was bad from the horrified expressions on everyone's faces. My dad jumped up and lifted me into his arms. He cleaned my wounds and wrapped huge bandages around my knees. He held and soothed me until I calmed down. I still have scars on my knees, reminding me of my father's loving-kindness.

If having the square for a playground was not enough, our other playground was the jail itself! That was a wonderland to a kid! When there were no prisoners we had full access, including the cells. That's where we loved to play. We would lock each other up or just explore. There were two small cells downstairs and one large cell upstairs with a smaller cell inside the larger cell. That was the one we had the most fun in. We had the best adventures.

I love to laugh. I love funny things. I guess that is one of the many reasons I feel so close to my dad. He loves practical jokes, so I get it from him! One day my dad locked us up in the upstairs cell. I remember thinking, *how are we going to get out of here?* The door to the cell was at the top of the stairs. We tried squeezing through the bars, but that didn't work. I looked at my sisters and then looked at the square opening that food for the prisoners was served through. I knew Yolanda would fit, but I worried about her falling down the stairs when she got on the other side. I looked at Leah. I wasn't sure about her shoulders. I thought, *if we can just get her shoulders through, we can be free!* She climbed up the bars and I helped guide her head through the square food opening. Next, we worked on one shoulder. *Got it!*

Then the other shoulder finally slipped through! We had done it! Once she got on the other side, she climbed down the bars, snuck downstairs, got the keys and set us free! Not too long after that, one of the dispatchers locked us up. He tricked us into going up there. When we got there, he quickly locked us in, laughing, pleased with himself that he "got" us. Little did he know that the joke was on him. This was now old hat to us. Once again, Leah was squeezing through to save her sisters! When we would be in the jail office and the dispatcher would walk away from the radio, I would run over, hit the button on the radio, and say, "Daddy? You out there?" Next thing you know, Dad would come on telling the dispatcher to get us off that radio. Maybe that's why the dispatcher tried locking us up!

My all time favorite practical joke was the "holes". Our bedroom was above the office of the jail. By one of the walls, there were several holes in the floor of our bedroom, which was the ceiling of the office. The holes were about a half an inch to an inch in size. One of the holes was above the doorway, and another hole was above Dad's desk. When we would go to our room for bed, we would slide our bunk beds out from the wall and peek through those holes. One day, we got the bright idea to get our water guns. Dad was sitting at his desk. We aimed those water guns through the hole and fired! It was a direct hit! My sisters and I laughed so hard. We stopped and peeked through the hole. Dad was looking around, so we shot another round. It was a while before he figured out what was going on. We got a lot of unsuspecting people in the office with those water guns.

There would be times, of course, when there were prisoners. When the prisoners were let out of the cells for good behavior, the ones Dad knew really well, they were the ones I learned card games from. Rummy was my favorite. The one I disliked the most was 52 card pick-up.

"Have you ever played 52 card pick-up?" The prisoner asked.

"No." I responded, eager to learn a new game. I loved cards. The next thing I knew, the cards were flying all over the place.

"Now, pick 'em up," he said. *Ugh!*

My dad loves baseball. He loves to watch it on the television. I, on the other hand, find it to be one of the most boring things to watch on T.V. I like going to a game, but not watching it on the television. I remember sitting in the office and watching a game, and other times curled up in his lap in the big recliner in our living room with a game on. No matter how boring I thought it was, I loved just being with him.

My dad love, love, loves his girls! That is one thing I have never doubted. I have never heard him complain or pine over the fact that he never had any boys. He did, however, pour everything that he would have poured into a son, right into his daughters. One of my favorite father-daughter times was going to the shooting range. I loved everything about it! I was a regular Annie Oakley!

Dad also taught us how to fight and how to protect ourselves. Little did I know how that was going to come in handy. I was in the third grade. We were out at recess. I was on the swings with my friends. The next thing I knew, a sixth grade boy came over from the blacktop to the playground, where he was not supposed to be. He started calling my dad all sorts of bad names. I was so upset. It turns out that my dad had arrested his dad. On and on he went with his taunts. He was a big kid, especially to a third grade girl. Finally, I could take no more and I punched him in the stomach. When he rose up, he punched me in the mouth. That's when I really let him have it. The moves I was taught and had practiced, came so easily, I did not even think about it. It was automatic. I had been told where to kick if a boy ever "tried" anything. Which at that age, I did not even know what that meant. I also did not know what really happened when I kicked there except that he would bend over and when he did, I was to grab his ears and bash his face with my knee, so, I did. I gave the hardest kick I could muster, when he doubled over, I grabbed his ears and bashed his face with my knee. Down he went for the count! When I got home, my mom was devastated.

"You should have turned the other cheek!"

By the time my dad got home, my lip was incredibly swollen.

Before he even learned what happened he said, "The other guy better look worse."

I smiled with my fat lip and told him all that had occurred.

"That's my girl!" he said.

I felt so proud of myself. No one picked on me or said bad things about my dad to my face after that. The only other thing that I was ever offended by was the song "I Shot the Sheriff" sung by Eric Clapton. I was never a fan of that song. Look out, Eric…

All my friends loved my dad. They got so excited when they were invited over. Everyone wanted to come to the jail to play. They also loved going for rides in his police car. He always made it so much fun for everyone.

Life of the sheriff's daughter wasn't all fun and games, though. There were many times when Dad would pick us up from school, or we would just be out with him, and he would get a call from the dispatcher. He would radio back that he had us girls. Dad would then think of someone on the way to the call where he could drop us off. The dispatcher would phone to see if they were home. If so, Dad would take us there and then speed off to his mission. I also remember being in the office, and hearing him come over the radio saying that he was bringing someone in. We would then have to leave. Sometimes the prisoners were belligerent and would start a fight with him. Down they would go.

The night that the jail was set on fire was scary! I remember Leah on the floor coloring. We had ordered a pizza. Of course, no one delivers all the way out to Lynchburg, so my mom and I went to pick it up. By the time we got back, the fire department was there hosing down the jail, and I saw flames coming up the side of the building.

I will never forget when the "hit" was put out on him. At the time, I did not know all the details of what was going on. I did not know that somebody wanted my daddy dead.

That night when my dad went missing—when the undercover agent took him to Chattanooga—was utter chaos. It was the middle of the night, and I awoke to a lot of noise and bright lights shining in my window. I had no idea what was going on. I heard my mom in the bedroom next to ours praying. She was crying out to God asking him to keep my daddy safe and bring him back home. That's when I got really scared. I walked over to the window and looked out. I had never seen so many police cars and officers all in one place. There were also T.V. news vans and newspaper people all over. I knew something was terribly wrong. I started crying, and I, too, like my mom, asked God to bring my daddy home, even though I did not know what was going on. I just knew he wasn't home and something wasn't right. I went to my parents' room and crawled in my mom's lap as she prayed. Suddenly, there was even greater commotion. We went downstairs and stood at the door, and then we saw him, my daddy! Mom went running out the door and they came in together. I had never felt so relieved and happy. We were up so late, so my mom said I did not have to go to school the next day. As far as I was concerned, things were just getting better and better! Then a newscaster with a big camera and bright lights came over and started asking my dad a bunch of questions.

She then looked at me and asked, "What do you think about all of this?"

With a big smile, I said, "I'm just happy my daddy's home and I don't have to go to school tomorrow!"

I loved growing up in the jail. The unique experience has given me memories I will always treasure. I love my dad. There's no doubt about it, I'm a Daddy's girl! And, of course, I'm his favorite, although, if you asked my sisters that, they would say they were his favorite as well. He has a way of making us all feel that way. When I first moved away from home, I missed my dad so much that I would turn the television on and find a baseball game just to hear it, so I could feel close to him. He has been a hero to many. His whole life has been dedicated to serving and protecting the community. He has laid his life on the line for people he knows and complete strangers without a second thought. To me, though, he's my dad. The man who would tuck me in at night and help me say my prayers. The man who taught me how to protect myself and to stand up for what is right. The man who showed me how to have fun with some of the best practical jokes. The man who picked me up when I was scared or hurt and kissed the pain away. My hero. My dad. I am so thankful to my heavenly Father for blessing me with such a wonderful dad. So thankful that He answered a little girl's prayer to bring her daddy home.

Leah

My face first pressed against the glass door: sad, lonely, longing to be old enough to join her...this is the first memory I can reach back and grasp. The year was 1976. I, Leah Dawn Cunningham, longed to join my sister Shannon in school. I remember watching her climb into the big yellow bus and feeling so lonely that I would spend the day without her. We lived in the jailhouse—yes, in the jailhouse in Lynchburg, Tennessee. As I recall, it seemed like such a big place. Our home was in one side and the jail in the other. Oddly enough, I can still recall the smells and sounds of that sweet old place. It was musty and always bustling with people. As you walked into this jailhouse you were facing a wall. If you chose to go to the right, you were in our home and to the left was the jail itself. You first entered our living room and around the corner was a staircase that led up to two bedrooms, one for our parents and one for the three girls. Downstairs past the living room was a bathroom and a dining area. Just beyond this lay the kitchen. Aw, the kitchen! Lots of memories here. I very much remember my mother making lunch for all the employees and prisoners. Often it was bologna sandwiches. I also remember standing on the kitchen counter just waiting for Dad to come by so I could pounce on him. Back at the entrance of the jail, if you chose to go to the left, you were in the office of the jailhouse. Around the corner there was a stairway that led up to several cells. At the back, downstairs, straight behind the office, were two more cells. This area also connected to the kitchen. Talking about it now, I smile and laugh about living in the jail, but at the same time, it seemed so normal. That was my life, and I loved it.

So, the first memories I have began here. An average day for me consisted of my dad pulling some silly prank on "his girls". He was silly and serious at the same time, and quite well-known for both traits. I remember Dad taking the handcuffs and cuffing my ankle to my sister Shannon's and sending us down to the market at the end of the street. I'm sure we were a sight to behold, trying to make our way, learning how to walk with "three legs". People would stop us and laugh and ask what we were doing, and we would simply say, "Daddy did it". And with a thorough understanding of my father they would just reply. "Aw, yep, that sounds like Ron." I learned early that it was going to become my goal to not let him think he "got me".

One time he locked Shannon and me in one of the upstairs cells. Back then the slots for sending the food through to the prisoners were of substantial size, I suppose. Shannon and I simply giggled as she pushed me through the food tray slot. I ran for the keys and released her, and then we ran to Dad, laughing with joy.

And oh, how I missed him while he was gone to work. I was not the type of kid to leave alone. Oh, no, all kinds of things could happen then! With Dad at work, Shannon at school and Mom making lunch for the prisoners or taking care of my new baby sister, Yolanda, I was left to my own devices a couple of times. What happened? Well, once I remember crawling up under the dispatch desk, mike in hand. I pushed the button I had seen the dispatcher push so many times before, and said, "Daddy, Daddy! When you comin' home?" I heard his sweet voice reply umm, not so sweetly, "Somebody get Leah off the radio". And one time I had a dresser I shared with my sisters Shannon and Yolanda that had a bookshelf at the top. I decided I needed something from that bookshelf, so I pulled the drawers out to use them like stairs to climb to the top. When I reached the bookshelf portion of the dresser, I realized it was not attached. Well, this realization came a little too late, and down I went, slamming into the floor, with the book case on top of my small body. I remember that one of the prisoners who was on the work release program heard the fall, ran up the stairs, and scooped me up in his arms until I caught my breath.

Oh, yes, I was quite the mischievous child. My sister and I shared a bunk bed and I remember rolling out of my bed one night and finding a hole in the floor of our room. Shannon and I could look down through that hole and see prisoners being brought in for booking. We would take water guns and shoot into the hole hoping to spray some random, unsuspecting soul. Then we would giggle forever, it seemed. But I will never forget Dad discovering our trick and yelling up the stairs in his powerful voice, "Girls, get in bed!" Well, round and round the kidding about this went for years, and, in fact, continues today.

There is one course of events which is not funny at all which I will never forget: the attempts on my dad's life. Now things can be a bit sketchy here for me. I was very young, but still, some of the events are oh, so clear. I most certainly remember the basics...someone in our small town put a contract out on my dad's life. I was with him on some of the occasions when these attempts were made.

One night, when I was about four years old, my mom and sisters had gone to pick up pizza and left me home with Dad. I remember lying on the floor in our living room coloring one of those giant coloring books. It was a Mickey Mouse book. At one point I realized the floor was really warm. I went into the dispatch office and told Dad and some of his ambulance drivers that he was talking to. They kindly patted me on the head and kindly assured me that everything was fine. I went back to my coloring for a few minutes, then realized that the floor was getting even hotter. l returned to the dispatch office and told them another time. Someone bent over and touched the floor. Agreeing with me, the commotion began. Next thing I know there are lots of people standing outside the jail, and my mother is running over and hugging me, asking me what was going on. Apparently, someone had tried to set a fire in the crawl space under the building.

Another night I remember we were driving home and someone tried to run us off the road. Dad told my sisters and me to get into the floor of the car. Shots were fired, and Dad was driving like a wild man. I remember that I was so scared that I was crying in the floor of that car.

Of course, I was but a child then. I know that there were many more attempts, and I am not sure that Dad even recalls every moment with vivid detail. I do recall the night that the F.B.I. staged my father's death. It is all somewhat vague to me, but I have heard the stories as an adult, and have been able to put two and two together. From my prospective that night, I remember my mother crying and others trying to console her. At that time, I was very confused as to what had happened, but I knew it was bad, and I will never forget crying myself to sleep in the confusion.

Yolanda

My memories as a child are probably the smallest of us girls, my being the baby. It also seems like I may have blocked some things from my mind while still dreaming about other things that happened back then. It all seems like it was so much drama and excitement, more than what most can say happened in their childhood. Certainly not just your normal raising up. I remember my dad had a lot of political conventions that he had to attend. I remember going to some of them as a family. One convention I recall was to benefit orphan children. I don't remember much about it, but I do remember that a picture was being taken of orphans for the newspaper, and for some reason, my sisters and I decided we wanted to be in the picture, too. From looking at the picture, it doesn't appear that we really wanted to be in it, though. Although we really fit in quite well with the orphans. Another convention which comes to mind was a sheriff's convention. My memories are just so vague of that time, with only parts which seem clear. Hee Haw guitars stick out to me. We were given them while we were there. We loved Hee Haw then. It was a great show to watch. I will never forget the bang on the door while we were playing with those guitars. The bang was sooo loud!!! It scared us all sooo very much that Dad wasn't there to protect us. He was in the sheriff's convention meeting downstairs in the hotel conference room. My mom had to call downstairs for help and I will never forget all of the men who ran upstairs to our room to come to our rescue. I do believe at one of those conventions that Al Gore was there, too. Him being from Tennessee, I remember him and Tipper being friends of our family's and being at some of the political conventions.

It was definitely unique living in a jail as a child. I will never forget when I used to ride my tricycle around the square. Back then we had a five and dime shop. This one old man, Peppers (the owner), who would always be walking around the square would always give me change, so I would ride my little tricycle to the five and dime shop and spend my change on candy. Always had to get something for my sisters, too. I can still smell the scent of cedar as older men would set around on the benches outside whittling their cedar sticks. When I smell cedar, even today, I think fondly of my hometown, Lynchburg.

I used to love "Frontier Days" when I was a little girl. I will never forget the fact that right where the gazebo is now they used to have ponies during Frontier Days. I could look out my window upstairs in the jailhouse where we lived, and there they were. I loved to ride those ponies. Another thing I won't ever forget is their smell. It's funny how a smell can bring back a memory. Whiskey and cedar are big smells that remind me of my childhood in Lynchburg. I loved riding the motorcycles that came through one year. It was the Hell's Angels. One year during Frontier Days when they came through town Daddy let me ride with them around the square. That was sooo much fun! My mom was sooo nervous. I also loved to sing on the square with my sisters. Local people would come just to listen to the sheriff's daughters sing on the stage during Frontier Days. That was such a big deal then.

This was awesome!!! Elvis came to town!!! Well, not really Elvis Presley. But he was the *great* Elvis impersonator, "Elvis Wade" Cummings. Even the real Elvis said he was great. He sang at the Lynchburg Elementary School, and stayed at the jail with us. I will never forget him taking a shower and me sitting at the door listening to him sing in the shower. He sounded just like Elvis. Looked just like him, too! To me he was identical!!!

One Christmas Shannon, Leah and I were so excited because Santa Claus was coming personally just to see us. We were all waiting impatiently. My dad was going to have this man come in dressed up as Santa, but for some reason it didn't work out, so my dad desperately need to find a Santa, and quick!!! He went upstairs to where the prisoners were, and there was this one big, jolly heavy man. My dad was thrilled, and had him dress up like Santa. So here we are now, sitting downstairs by the Christmas tree waiting, when all of a sudden, we hear the sound of feet coming down those wooden steps, and we hear this deep "Ho, ho, ho!" All three of us girls get up and pop, pop, pop our heads up past the wall and gaze up the staircase to see this big ole black man dressed up as Santa Claus. Our eyes really got wide, and we all three yelled at the same time, "Daddy, he's black!!!" That man laughed till he cried, and so did our dad. It was a cherished moment which will forever stay with me.

Shannon, Leah and I shared a room. Shannon and Leah had the bunk beds, and my bed was off to itself by the wall. The room right under us was Daddy's office, where he worked a lot of the time. There was a hole in our floor. We loved it. That hole became very entertaining for us when we got bored. We would fill our water guns and squirt the deputies in the head as they would walk by. Then we would peep down the hole and watch them look up, wondering what it was that was falling and getting them wet, as they wiped their heads with their hands. Sometimes we would drop a stick through that hole and bonk one of them on the head. Someone must have found out what we were doing, because one day one of them filled up the hole with something. Oh, well! It was fun while it lasted.

Back then everything was sooo much different than it is now. Today, little girls would never be out just driving around with their dad in his patrol car, but back then, we could, and did sometimes in the town of Lynchburg. I will never forget one night my dad had a call and Shannon, Leah and I were all together in the back seat. Dad was out driving around just checking things out. All of a sudden there were shots being fired at my dad's sheriff car! All I can remember is him yelling for us to get down! The driver of the car that the shots were coming from just slammed on his brakes, and turned right in front of us and the shooting started. There were bullet holes all the way down the side of my dad's car. Angels were definitely with us, 'cause no one was hit or hurt at all.

My dad has had to answer many calls that have been difficult on him and my family. I have witnessed a lot and endured a lot of hardship, but have also had many great experiences that no other children besides us girls can say they have had. My childhood probably had a bigger impact on me than either of my sisters, even though they can remember more of this time period than I do, since I am the youngest. There was just so much I could not understand about why this or that was happening. A lot of it is fuzzy to me. I do remember though that I had, and still have, a very brave dad, of whom I am extremely proud. He has overcome so much. Through the time he was sheriff, yes, there were lots of ups and downs, and strange things took place, but he is still here today, and standing tall. So am I—as a very proud daughter.

I used to love to let certain prisoners play Barbies with me when I was bored and couldn't get anyone else to play with me. Sad, right?

It's just that all of the memories I have of my childhood seem so big, and now when I go back to visit the small town of Lynchburg, everything seems so small. I used to think our house was so big...and our bedroom. Now when I go up to the room, in what is now a museum, it is so little. I can't believe I ever thought it was big. The same goes for Lynchburg Elementary playground. I have driven by it and thought to myself, *wow, this isn't big at all!*

The problems that resulted in my family because of the conspiracy against my dad really affected everyone. The tension was so hard for me as a child. I was Daddy's girl no matter what, and could not understand how things like these affected adults. We ended up moving. My mom had to work a lot then. I'll never forget when I had a babysitter who had to watch us and I decided to pretend to run away. Well, that consisted of hiding under a bed with my stuffed animals around me so I could not be seen—so I thought. My babysitter called my dad at work to tell him she couldn't find me. He had to come out to the house looking for me. Somehow he knew right where to go. I'll never forget seeing those big black boots...then they stopped. Then my daddy bent down and there he was, looking at me. My eyes and mouth were starting to quiver, 'cause I knew what was coming. He pulled me out from under the bed and sat me on it. He was slowly pulling out his belt. His eyes started filling up with tears as he said, "Honey, you know why I have to do this, don't you?" I looked right into my daddy's eyes and said, "Yes, Daddy, because you love me." After that, he couldn't do it. That was a hard moment for him and for me. My heart and his heart already felt broken. That was truly a difficult time then, but I know now that a father/daughter love is unconditional.

CO-AUTHOR NOTES

Working with Ron on the original book, *Conspiracy in the Town that Time Forgot* and this sequel have been some of my best experiences to date in my role as an author. As in the first book, some names are changed to protect the innocent.

Our original work was a regional best-seller, was featured on *Tullahoma Living* on cable TV Channel Six, and in a number of newspapers. It was extremely well received by the law enforcement and legal communities, and was granted great reviews by the media, authors, attorneys and business professionals. It found its way into libraries and archives in several states, and was listed as an Amazon "hot new release."

The more I have gotten to know this extraordinary individual, the more I have come to realize what a hero he really was and still is today. The career of law enforcement, in itself, is a noble and high calling, and takes an especially dedicated and talented professional to adequately fulfill its duties.

Since the beginning of Ron's exceptional career, he has proven to be a fearless and determined officer who has endured numerous personal attacks and challenges, and come forth a victor.

This title not only sheds further light on the conspiracy story, but delves into a number of new cases which Ron handled during his term as Sheriff of Moore County, Tennessee, which were not presented in the first book, and allows the reader to see inside a true hero.

Even today Ron, as much as ever, faces daily challenges in his current position as Investigative Captain of the Tullahoma, Tennessee Police Department.

I have a personal friend who is a British nobleman, and recently attended an event at which a senior member of the royal family was present. I have met a US president (before his election to that post), other icons in the American political world and the speaker of the Canadian House of Commons. I have had one-on-one conversations with a nationally renowned football star, several idols in the musical world and even had the great privilege of meeting and shaking the hand of the late legendary General Jimmy Doolittle. Many of these noteworthy individuals are certainly heroes in the eyes of the world. But Ron, you are not only my best friend, you are my distinctive hero.

Stan St. Clair

RON'S INTRODUCTION

This morning I was asked by a friend to have a cup of coffee with him. As we were having a conversation, two of his friends came and sat down. He introduced me by asking them if they knew me. They answered, "No". He said, "This is Ron Cunningham—you know, the one just came out with the book where someone tried to kill him when he was Sheriff of Moore County." One man said he lived in Moore County and remembered when it happened. As I sat there listening, he explained that he had bought the book and read it. The next thing he asked me was, "When are you going to make a sequel? You should make a movie."

I am proud to say that I was Sheriff of Moore County during the '70s and '80s. I am proud to be a member of law enforcement and Captain of Investigation for the City of Tullahoma,

Tennessee. It has been my chosen profession for over thirty years. I have not gotten rich, but it has been good to me and I love it. I am sure all law enforcement officers have an experience they could share. This is mine.

I am just glad that God was on my side and the alleged intended killers were not better shots and I am still alive. So I am attempting to turn back the clock and tell some more of many experiences. Buy a book, grab a cup of coffee and take a ride with me back into the past. Fasten your seat belt and hold on, because here we go!

CHAPTER ONE

Night concedes quietly to the dawn as it comes slipping over sleepy rural villages all over the South. Lynchburg was no different. On a normal morning the only sound heard at sunrise is the crowing of roosters on the nearby farms scattered across Moore County, Tennessee. This familiar alarm is soon joined by the incessant barking of countless farm dogs which wakens the remaining households. One by one lights start appearing in windows and those within are rousing to the tantalizing aroma of fresh-brewed coffee and preparing to meet another day.

The brisk morning breeze outside was carrying the ambrosial odor of mash cooking at Jack Daniel's Distillery. Everything *seemed* normal. But it wasn't this morning. Not in Lynchburg. And certainly not for Sheriff Ron Cunningham.

It had been a long, sleepless night for the sheriff. A year-long state and federal investigation into a sinister plot to take his life had culminated in the arrest of three people. The death of the sheriff had been faked in order to ensnare those involved in the conspiracy. Two had been arrested at the East Ridge Sheraton Inn at Chattanooga, where they had entered a rented room so they could have an alibi for being out of Lynchburg when the murder took place. The third was taken at his home in Lynchburg.

Though Ron was acutely aware that more individuals were involved, he had agreed to cut the investigation short due to the mass confusion which he had been told was taking over in the town of Lynchburg.

As Ron sat pensively in the back seat of the unmarked patrol car bringing him home, along with the legendary Lacy "Moon" Brown and the TBI agents, he wondered if he had made the most advantageous decision. The past year's events buzzed through his head. The shots fired at him on various occasions, the attempt to burn the jail in which he and his family lived.

As the cruiser turned left at the only traffic light in town and the first rays of light broke through the early-morning haze, it became obvious that the square was a beehive of activity, swarming with law enforcement officers, search and rescue teams, and of course, the ever-present media. Ron sighed deeply. He knew he had made the proper choice, indeed.

As his car door eased open, he was immediately barraged. Ron would finally be able to return to his shaken family. But his rest would be short-lived. Life could never be the same, and would certainly never be taken for granted again. The pursuit of justice must now commence.

**The late undercover legend,
Lacy "Moon" Brown**

Photo property of Ron Cunninhgam

CHAPTER TWO

Ron was groggy from lack of sleep. Reporters and journalists, not only local and from adjoining states, but some from as far away as Michigan, crowded the square and the area in front of his office.

One even stuck some papers in his face and bluntly commanded, "Sign this". What for? Movie rights, book rights, etc. What would Ron get in return? Nothing. The sheriff was not dumb, by any means. Just dumb-struck and overly sleepy.

"You'll have to work that out with my lawyer," Ron replied coolly.

Pushing his way through the throng, Ron entered the building to encounter more of the same. Steve Hanley, the jailer / dispatcher, was busily answering the phone and taking messages. "How is the sheriff? Is he hurt? Is he okay? Tell him to call me as soon as he can." David Maynard, the chief deputy, was there. He had been temporarily appointed as sheriff earlier that morning by the county executive. Ron's stunned family members, including his three impressionable young daughters, Shannon, Leah and Yolanda, were there, along with numerous friends. Ron dutifully answered questions and made statements to the press, as he steadily grew wearier. As the crowd finally dispersed, he made his way to his bed and hopefully, some well-deserved repose.

But sleep did not come easy for him that morning. He tossed and turned restlessly, as the previous night's activities kept interrupting his rest.

The investigation of the plot to murder the sheriff had been ongoing for at least a year. So obviously, others had also wanted him out of the picture. On several occasions he had been notified by undercover agents and various agencies that they were setting up buys for stolen property, guns and drugs. The higher authorities were dead-set on accumulating as much evidence as possible against these people. Dates had previously been set for the murder to take place, and then it had been called off for varying reasons. Attempts had been made on his life on several occasions. After a number of local attempts, they had hired an undercover cop to do the job. But this time he finally had some control over it.

That night Ron had gotten the call that the deal was finally going to go down. "Meet us behind the high school at 9:00," the caller had said somberly. "My name is Shooter, and I will have someone else with me. We'll be driving a 1976 maroon Chevy Impala. I'll be wearing blue jeans and a leather jacket. The other guy will be wearing a gray three-piece suit."

Feeling a bit nervous, apprehensive and alone, and knowing that someone truly wanted him dead, the sheriff began preparing himself. First he contacted a couple of persons whom he knew he could trust and told them he was going to meet someone and would be accompanying them to Chattanooga East Ridge Sheraton Hotel, in case anything went wrong. Then he radioed the deputy on duty and told him he was checking out a car behind the high school. He would be doubly prepared for any mishap.

Ron then armed himself with a .357 magnum Colt Python, a Colt .38 Featherweight and a .380 Lama automatic, fully loaded with extra ammunition. He wore loose-fitting jeans, a long-sleeved shirt, a light leather jacket and heavy socks with light shoes. As ready as he could ever be under the unsettling circumstances, he kissed his family goodbye, hopped in his cruiser, and headed for the high school.

As he approached the rear of the building, he could see the maroon Impala and a couple of white males standing beside it. The sheriff parked his car where it would be between him and the two strangers, then got out.

"Get in the back seat." The voice was the one called "Shooter".

Ron obliged, scooted over behind the driver's seat, then slipped his hand into his jacket and removed the .380. The guy with the suit was now on the passenger's side.

"Sheriff, what is the best way to get out of here back to the interstate?" Shooter asked.

Thinking quickly, the sheriff gave him directions that soon had them lost. Ron felt that he now had an advantage. He had them where they had no idea of their location, and he had the .380 pointing at the back of the driver's head. He could take him out, if need be, and have a chance at the passenger.

"I know what you're doing Sheriff," Shooter said, "and I don't blame you. But we're working on a time schedule, and have to be back in Chattanooga soon or they might get suspicious."

At least this made sense. Ron eased the gun down and led them back to Tullahoma and to the AEDC Road which took them to Interstate 24. But he would keep his hand on the .380 inside his jacket—pointed at the driver's head.

CHAPTER THREE

As they were driving up Monteagle Mountain, Shooter calmly turned to "Three Piece". "Maybe we should fire a shot out the window, just in case." Three Piece agreed. Shooter rolled down his window, took his weapon in hand, and fired a shrill shot into the blackness of night. Just as Shooter's gun spoke, Ron pulled the trigger of the .380. Equally as quickly, out of the instinct which had sustained his life, his thumb caught the hammer before it could strike the firing pin. Ron was sweating profusely. He let out his breath slowly and realized that he had been holding it for an indeterminate time.

As the Impala cruised into the city limits of Chattanooga, Shooter exited and entered a truck stop and broke the eerie silence. "Let's go get something to drink." Ron knew the drama was reaching a climax, and his throat was as dry as a parched desert. A Coke would certainly be a welcome relief. As the light swept over the passenger, Ron recognized "Three Piece".

After they had gotten their drinks and were returning to the car Ron spoke. "I remember you from Investigation School. I guess I can relax a little now." He was none other than Inspector Huckabee with the TBI.

"Yeah. I was there." Huckebee nodded.

"I need your .357 for proof of the deed. And your wallet with your badge and ID," Shooter said.

Ron obliged. "I hope that's all. I just want this to be over."

"Na, there's one other thing I promised to bring."

"What's that?"

"One of your ears." Shooter spoke matter-of-factly.

"You're sure as the dickens not getting one of my ears!"

Shooter managed a hint of a smile. "I think I can handle that problem."

Ron showed him the .380 and the Featherweight, and told him about pulling the trigger when he had fired the shot out the window. He figured that honest confession was "good for the soul".

Shooter slammed his car door, and pulled toward the interstate. "Man, that's as close as I've ever come to getting shot since I've been doing undercover work."

As they were nearing the East Ridge Sheraton, a two-way radio crackled, and a voice squawked excitedly, "Farmer to Shooter, Farmer to Shooter! One of the cows is out! I repeat, one of the cows is out!"

Shooter did a bootleg turn, and sped down the highway away from the hotel. Within a few minutes, the radio crackled again. "Farmer to Shooter, Farmer to Shooter! The cow is back in. You have an all-clear."

While pulling into the hotel, Inspector Huckabee informed the sheriff that they were going to drop him off at the back door. He would be met by another agent who would take him upstairs to his room. The entire hotel was being controlled by their team.

When Ron emerged, there was no agent. After waiting what seemed an eternity, he heard footsteps tapping down the stairs, and he quickly backed under the stairwell. In a flash, the wiry sheriff was upon the figure, thrusting an arm around his throat, and jamming a gun under his chin!

The shaken stranger stiffened. "Are you Ron?" he asked, trying to veer his eyes toward his captor.

The sheriff nodded. "Yes."

"I'm supposed to take you upstairs."

Ron let out a muffled sigh.

"Let me see some ID."

The agent slipped his hand into his jacket pocket and jerked out a badge.

"Okay," Ron grunted. "Let's go."

CHAPTER FOUR

The agent slowly led Ron up the stairs to the second floor. Just to the left, as they entered the hallway, a door opened as if by prearrangement, and the sheriff was ushered in, a headset being instantly thrust into his hands. As he pulled them over his ears, someone silently pointed to a TV monitor.

Clint Rivers was sitting at a small table by the window. On the table was a McDonald's hamburger sack with a handgun next to it. Rivers' wife, Nona, was sitting on the bed chowing down on a burger. Spread over the length and breadth of the bed was an impressive assortment of guns. Leaning against the wall nonchalantly stood Shooter, his right foot on the wall, itself, his knee bent outward.

"I need my bucks, man! I need my bucks!" Shooter snapped adamantly. "I need to be out of here before someone finds his body!"

Rivers stuck out his hand toward Shooter. "The gun?"

Shooter reached behind him and pulled the sheriff's .357 from his belt, laying it in Rivers' hand.

"The badge?"

Shooter plunged his hand into his jacket pocket and retrieved Ron's wallet.

"That's great. You really got his wallet." Looking inside, he saw the badge and driver's license, and managed a smile. "He even left $300.00!"

Nona buried her head in her hands and cried, "We really did it! Oh, well, I'm glad it's over!"

Rivers extended his hand one last time. "Okay, give it to me."

"What?" Shooter yipped, knowing the answer.

"The ear—that was the deal!"

"Oh, that." Shooter laughed. "I was cutting off his ear and a car was coming, and I had to throw him in the river. I need my bucks so I can get out of here before they find the body."

Rivers and Nona were laughing about the ear incident. "I guess we have enough proof, but I'll have to call James to okay it."

"You got anything to drink?" Shooter asked Rivers.

"Just some Jack Daniel's. No ice or Coke."

"Tell ya what. I'll go get some ice and Coke while you get my bucks okayed."

Shooter left the room.

CHAPTER FIVE

Ron saw the door ease open as Shooter entered. The room was filled with agents. The undercover legend, Lacy "Moon" Brown, who had been so instrumental in bringing this sting down, the FBI agents, and other officers.

The phone rang. It was Jim Parrott, the TBI agent assigned to Lynchburg and Moore County.

"All hell has broken loose down here. Someone found the sheriff's car behind the high school, and they say they found some blood in it. Every sheriff's office and police department around has somebody down here. They've shut down all the roads and are searching for the sheriff. The square is full of reporters and TV crews. There is total chaos down here!"

Ron was immediately informed of the situation in Lynchburg. He was also told that they are aware that others are involved in the plot to have him killed.

"I know you want to catch all of them," Huckabee said. "We are with you. We want to get them all. But it's up to you. The ball is in your court."

"Is there enough evidence to convict these three?" Ron said thoughtfully.

The agents looked at one another. "Yes," said Huckabee, "we all agree. We've got them red-handed."

"Okay, let's wrap this up and get back to Lynchburg as soon as possible."

Shooter returned to Rivers' room with Moon. His knock was answered by Nona.

While Shooter walked over to Rivers, Moon stood by the bed. Shooter sat the ice and Coke on the table.

"Hey, man. You get the okay for my bucks?"

Rivers handed Shooter $5,000.00. "It's all there. All in hundreds."

Suddenly Shooter pulled a handgun and stuck it under Rivers' chin. In a flash, Rivers plunged toward the gun on the table.

"Don't do it, man!" Shooter yelled.

Nona reached for a handgun from the bed. Moon put a gun up to her ear before she had a grasp on her weapon.

"Don't," Moon said authoritatively.

Agent Wix suddenly burst into the room.

"Clinton Rivers, Nona Rivers, you are under arrest for conspiracy to commit murder and solicitation to take a human life. Cuff 'em!"

The couple was read their rights. Ron entered the room.

"I think you know this man," Agent Wix said.

"Yeah, I know Ron." Rivers stuck out his hand toward the sheriff. "I hope you don't have any hard feelings."

Ron's blood pressure skyrocketed. He felt as if all of his blood was running to his head. He clinched his fist and stepped toward Rivers.

Agent Wix grabbed Ron's arm. "No, Ron! You're on video."

Ron had been tossing all day. The sordid memories had wrecked his attempts at rest. Could he possibly have to deal with anybody?

The phone must be answered. He looked at the clock. It was 4:30 PM.

Ron back in Lynchburg the morning after the sting to capture the conspirators

CHAPTER SIX

"Sheriff, it's me, Steve. I hate to have to bother you, but we've got an emergency on Tanyard Hill. Bobby Joe's drunk and out of control. Even his parents can't do anything with him. He's got a fencepost and is whipping everyone in sight. They told him they were going to call the sheriff, but he said he didn't care who they called. He said, 'I ain't afraid of no sheriff.' By the way, I'm dang sure glad you're alive!"

"Me too. That's okay, Steve, about bothering me. I can't sleep anyway."

Ron pulled into the driveway leading up to Bobby Joe's house. Sure enough, there he stood, out in the middle of the yard. In has big hands was a large locust fencepost. He was holding it like a batter about to wale a baseball, daring anyone to get close to him. Ron stepped out of his cruiser and walked over to Bobby Joe's parents.

"We can't do anything with him, Sheriff. He just won't listen. What are you gonna do?" his dad said.

"I'm going to try to get that fencepost away from him first, and see if I can talk some sense into him. If that doesn't work, I'll have to take him to jail."

"Do what you gotta do, Sheriff, but be careful. He won't listen to anybody. He's mean drunk."

As the sheriff eased toward Bobby Joe, he kept his eye glued on the fence post.

"You need to put that thing down, Bobby Joe, so we can talk."

"Go ahead and talk, but I ain't goin' to jail, Sheriff. I'll keep my post."

Bobby Joe was unsteady, but Ron could sense that he was dangerous. As he got closer, he saw the young man's grip tighten around the massive post. The sheriff ducked just as the post began to swing near his head. Plunging like a linebacker in the Super Bowl, Ron tackled his opponent and the fight was on. Wrestling the heavy post away, he was finally able to clamp the handcuffs on. But during the brief moments he was loading Bobby Joe into the back of the cruiser Ron's shirt was torn half off.

Bobby Joe laid down in the back seat and kicked, knocking out the right rear window. By the time Ron arrived with him at the jail, he had also managed to kick out the other rear window, the screen between the seats had been jarred loose, and two perfect boot marks were imprinted on the ceiling. Getting his prisoner from the car to the jail wore out the muscular sheriff.

Ron took a much-needed shower, and changed clothes. After supper, he helped his girls with homework and saying their prayers, then put them to bed, and headed for his own.

This time he slept like a baby.

CHAPTER SEVEN

On the morning of Friday, February 16th, 1979, after Clint and Nona Rivers were arrested in Chattanooga, while Ron was restlessly reliving his horrid night, Earl James was picked up at his home in Lynchburg. He received the same charges as the Rivers's. Unfortunately, the alleged conspirators were quick to make bond.

Ron was appalled.

He had been told that James was offering vital information of importance against the ex-governor in return for a plea bargain. But what about the safety of his family?

Time seemed to drag like a lame foot marking the sand along the path of his life. Each day was another move in the great game of chess which would determine his fate, and that of the players in the plot to take his life.

It was early March and the buttercups were popping up around Lynchburg. The aroma of coffee accosted Ron's nose, informing him that Steve was already in the office. Even though the morning was pleasant for that time of year, hot coffee was a ritual that Ron was not willing to forgo.

"Morning, Steve, what's up?"

"Not much, Sheriff. It's been pretty quiet around here this morning. Rusty called a few minutes ago. Wants you to come by and see him when you get a chance. He thinks he may have found a house for you."

"Really? Did he say where?"

"No. Just you need to come by and see him."

Ron felt that moving his family out of the jail was not necessarily the best way to protect them, but Linda wanted out. Granted, living in a jail was not like having a home of your own; but the jail *was* comfortable, and more importantly, free. Rearing a family on a law enforcement income was not easy—especially with three girls. But Ron decided he would at least go and see what his friend, Rusty Redd, had in mind.

Ron had started out the door on his way to Rusty's when the phone rang. Steve picked up.

"Yes sir, he's here. Do you need to speak with him?" There was a brief pause. "Sure, I'll tell him. I'm sorry to hear it."

Ron got the feeling that his plans would have to wait.

"That was Mr. Richard. Said his house had been broken into. He and his wife had just gotten back from New York and found the side door kicked in and some things missing."

"I guess I'd better go see about this. I'll go by Rusty's later. Knowing Mr. Richard, he'd expect me there five minutes ago."

Graddy Richard, CEO of the distillery, lived a few miles west of Lynchburg. His home, perched atop a majestic hill, was a huge, two-story brick colonial. The kind of place you'd expect the CEO of Jack Daniel's to live in. Cruising up the long driveway, Ron couldn't help but notice that the Bradford pears had bloomed, lining the driveway like two rows of white sentinels. Behind the stately white Bradfords, the forsythias were blossoming in yellow wild abandon. Hopefully a sure sign that the long, cold and miserable winter had finally surrendered all to sweet spring.

Ron approached the home slowly, instinctively looking for any clues the perp might have unwittingly left behind. As he stepped onto the porch Mr. Richard swung open the massive front door and invited him in.

"Sorry this happened to you," Ron said in a meaningful tone.

"I just want you to see what a mess that nut-job made of my home," Richard barked.

Whoever had broken in had certainly ransacked the interior. Drawers were pulled out, papers strewn all over. Jewelry and money scattered about. Mrs. Richard was busy trying to straighten up, picking up jewelry and shifting papers. Ron quickly intervened.

"If you don't mind, leave everything where it is. I need to get some pictures of the crime scene. Do you have any idea what's missing?" Ron said.

The Richards looked at each other.

"I'll need a list of everything you can think of. You can start working on it while I take pictures of this mess."

Ron returned to his car for his camera while Richard began listing the missing items. The process was not difficult. The intruder seemed to know exactly what he wanted. A sizable assemblage of guns and a collection of rare coins had been taken. After snapping a number of photos and meticulously dusting for prints, Ron set out to canvass the few neighbors in the area.

There were no close neighbors, the area being quite rural and sparsely populated with sprawling farms. However, upon questioning a few people who were home, one elderly lady told the sheriff that she had noticed a white van driving up and down the road, turning around in driveways the previous afternoon.

As Ron continued his house-to-house quest, one man also told him that he had a suspicious white van creeping around the neighborhood as he was driving toward town. According to this witness, the van had turned around at the state garage on Highway 50. After thanking the man, Ron headed for the garage.

As he pulled into the drive, he spotted Randy Arnold emerging from under a state dump truck.

"Hey, Randy! You got a minute? I need to ask you a few questions."

Randy had been known to smoke an occasional weed. "Why? Am I in trouble?"

"No, Randy. This isn't about you. Were you working yesterday?"

"Yeah. I was here all day." Randy's demeanor reflected the fact that he was still a bit wary of the purpose of the sheriff's unannounced visit.

"Did you see a white van hanging around here?"

"A white van?" Randy scratched his head and frowned. "As a matter of fact, I did. It pulled in the drive and turned around a couple of times. I just figured the driver was lost, since he wasn't from around here."

"How do you know that?"

"Because there was the name of a plumbing company on the side and it wasn't local."

"Do you remember the name of it?"

"No, but I thought it was kinda strange he was goin' up and down the road, so the last time he pulled in here I got his tag number."

A light seemed to shine from Ron's eyes. "Great! Can you get it for me?"

"Yeah, it's in the shop. Hold on, I'll get it."

When Randy returned Ron radioed Steve and asked him to run the number and call him back.

CHAPTER EIGHT

Barely five minutes had passed when Steve radioed back. The van was registered to a small plumbing business in Smyrna, Tennessee, just south of Nashville. Smyrna, at that time, was a bedroom community for commuters to Nashville, and was about seventy-five miles northwest of Lynchburg. Before making the trip, Ron thought it wise to return to the office and call the number Steve had gotten from information and see what he could learn.

"Hey, this is Ron Cunningham. I'm the sheriff down here in Moore County. Do you own a white van, and would you tell me your name please?"

"Yeah. Name's Ronnie Thurman. And I have a white van I use in my plumbing business, why?

"Do you know where it is now?"

"Not really. My nephew has it."

"What's his name?"

"Barry Price. He's my sister's boy."

"Any idea where he might be?"

"Well, he's working at a grocery store in Shelbyville and stays here most of the time when he's not working."

"What store?"

"He's working at Bi-Rite out on Murfreesboro Highway. Hey, Sheriff, what's this about? Is he in any trouble?"

"I don't know. I just want to talk to him."

Ron turned to Steve as he placed the phone back on the hook. "Let's get some lunch and then I'm going up to Shelbyville and see if I can locate this Barry Price and the white van."

After locking up the office, Steve and Ron strolled over to the White Rabbit Saloon. Upon seeing the pair enter, Jake, the proprietor, came over to take their orders.

"The usual for me, Jake," Ron said. "I've got to get up to Shelbyville in a few minutes. The Richards' house was broken into and I've got a lead I want to follow up on."

"That's a lucky break. By the way, what have you heard from the sheriff in Chattanooga? Any idea when you'll go to court?"

"I go tomorrow. The case against Rivers and James goes to the Grand Jury."

"Well, Sheriff, I sure hope they get those bastards. I knew that James was no good. I never trusted Rivers either."

The front door opened and a young couple entered the White Rabbit.

"It seems I need to get to work. They look like tourists. I need to pour on the Southern hospitality. Talk to you later."

"Right, Jake, see you later."

Ron and Steve finished eating and walked back across the square to the office.

"I'm hitting the road," Ron said, "I'll be back in a couple of hours. Call me on the radio if anything comes up while I'm gone. The Richards will be coming by this afternoon with a list and approximate value of what was taken. Tell them I have a good lead I'm following up on. I'll let them know if I have anything."

"Sure thing, Sheriff. Anything else?"

"No, just keep it quiet. See you later."

Ron pulled out from the office, drove around the east side of the square and turned right on highway 55 toward Tullahoma. At 41A he made a left turn and drove north toward his destination. Shelbyville, located about twenty miles north of Tullahoma, was best known for the annual walking horse celebration. During this busy event, the entire town became one large traffic jam. Ron was thankful the celebration was in September, and not now, or it would take an hour to get through town rather than the usual fifteen minutes. Even without the big surge in traffic, Shelbyville was not an easy town to drive through. Two-lane traffic and a light on every corner made even today slow going for a sheriff in a hurry. Finally making it to the inter-section where KFC sat on the corner, Ron made the right turn onto Murfreesboro Road and started looking for the Bi-Rite Grocery.

As he eased into the parking lot, Ron's eyes scanned it for any sign of the white van. It was nowhere in sight. After entering the store, the sheriff ID'd himself and asked for the manager.

"He's in his office in the back. I'll call him for you. Rick, there's a sheriff from Lynchburg here and he wants to talk to you." The cashier turned to Ron, "Go on back through the door that says 'employees only'. His office is the first door on the right."

Ron walked through the double doors to the back and spotted the door labeled "office". A middle-aged man sat at a desk with a small sign bearing the name "Ricky Atkins, manager".

Rick stood and extended his hand.

"Hi, I'm the sheriff of Moore County. I'm working on a robbery. Does Barry Price work here?"

"Well, Sheriff, he did until a short while ago. Came in asking for his pay and quit."

"How long ago?'

"About an hour ago, I guess."

Feeling a little frustrated at having been alluded by Price, Ron radioed back to Steve.

"Price isn't here. I missed him by about an hour. I'm thinking I'll go to Smyrna and see if I can catch him at his uncle's. Anything happening there?"

"Not much. Mr. Richard came with the list of his missing items. He listed an antique gun collection and an old coin collection. Says it was all worth about five thousand dollars."

"No surprises there. Thanks a lot, Steve. I'm headed for Smyrna. Maybe I'll get lucky. Call the house for me and tell Linda where I'm going and tell her I don't know when I'll be back. It depends on what I find there."

"Right, Sheriff. I'll call her right now. See you when you get back."

CHAPTER NINE

When Ron arrived at Ronnie Thurman's house, the van was there. Thurman answered the door.

"Hello, I'm Sheriff Ron Cunningham from Lynchburg. We talked on the phone."

"Sure. I remember."

"Is your nephew here?"

"No, he just left. He moved out."

"Do you mind if I come in?"

"No. Come on in."

"Where has he been staying while he was here?"

"In the back bedroom on the left."

"Do you mind if I take a look in the room?"

"No. What's he done?"

"Well, we think he broke into a house and stole some guns."

"How do you know it was him?"

"We don't know for sure, but your van was seen in the area, and someone got the tag number. You told me he was driving your van. Do either of you know anyone in Lynchburg?"

"No…not that I'm aware of."

A look through the bedroom revealed nothing of interest. On the way out, Ron spotted some guns in the living room, along with numerous coffee cans filled with coins.

"Mr. Thurman, who do these guns and coins belong to?"

"Oh, I'm a collector. They're mine."

Upon reaching his cruiser, Ron radioed the Rutherford County Sheriff's office and asked for an investigator to meet him at the Thurman house. Upon his arrival the officer informed Ron that Thurman was a "fence", a legal term for a receiver of stolen goods.

After questioning Thurman extensively, Ron asked permission to examine the guns. A check of the serial numbers revealed that they matched guns from the Richards' list. Ron informed Thurman that if he didn't tell him the truth he would be charged with receiving and concealing stolen property.

Upon this, Thurman relented and admitted purchasing some of the guns and coins from his nephew, Barry Price.

Afterward, a statement was taken by Ron and the Rutherford County investigator, and the list thoroughly checked from the Richards' house. All of the missing guns and coins were accounted for and recovered.

Ron then obtained Price's date of birth and Social Security number from his uncle, loaded up the recovered goods, and gave Thurman a receipt.

"Where was your nephew going from here?"

"Well, I think he was moving to Mobile, Alabama."

When the sheriff got back to Lynchburg with the recovered property, he called Graddy Richard and asked him to come in and retrieve it.

Richard, though glad to get back his guns and coins, was intent on apprehension of the thief.

"I'll give you $5,000 for the arrest and conviction of that young hoodlum!"

"I'll give it all I've got, Mr. Richard. But I've got a prior appointment. Steve, can you be here early in the morning? I have to go to Chattanooga for the arraignment of my woulda-been killers."

"Sure, Sheriff. I won't let you down."

CHAPTER TEN

The next morning Ron awoke to a seasonally warm, but rainy, March day, grabbed a hearty breakfast with plenty of coffee, and set off for the city.

When he arrived at the courthouse he was met by Lacy "Moon" Brown, Phil "Shooter" McCarty and agent Steve Worsham from the ATF, as well as District Attorney Gary D. Gerbitz of Hamilton County.

After testifying before the Federal Grand Jury of Criminal Court, the group gathered for lunch and received instructions to return at 1:00 P.M. During their lunch break they all agreed to meet at the sheriff's office in Lynchburg at a later date, where they would be treated to a tour of Jack Daniel's Distillery, and lunch at Ms. Mary Bobo's.

Upon returning to the courtroom, they were informed that the Grand Jury had indicted the Rivers' and Earl James on the two charges: conspiracy and solicitation to commit murder.

The petition stated that they, "along with divers other persons known and unknown to the Grand Jury by name, did unlawfully and feloniously combine, agree together and conspire together and with each other to procure, hire and solicit another person or persons to commit the murder of Ron Cunningham, Sheriff of Moore County, Tennessee…"

But the case was far from over. A date was set for the trio to go to court.

As the sheriff drove down I-24 west toward Lynchburg, he was contemplating a plan of action on catching Barry Price. By the time of his arrival, the plan had been formulated.

The next morning, the plan would go into action!

After breakfast, Ron called the Mobile, Alabama Police Department and spoke to an investigator, giving him the vitals on the suspect. He informed him that there was a $5,000 reward offered. But to top it off, the sheriff added an extra incentive: a case of Jack Daniel's Whisky to anyone giving information leading to Price's arrest and conviction.

Ron had gone down early to make the call. The familiar sound of hinges told him his dispatcher had arrived.

"Good morning, Steve. Beautiful day shaping up. Hey, I'm going to run out to see Rusty Redd. If you remember, you had just told me he had found a house for me when all this mess started with Barry Price."

"Yeah. I wondered when you'd ever get out there." Steve smiled and flopped down in his seat.

"I'll be back in a little bit. Call me on the radio if you need me."

Ron never ceased to enjoy the relaxing drive out to Redd's Grocery. It was one of his favorite places in the county. And seeing his old friend, Rusty, was always a pleasure. It was a favorite gathering place, and everyone felt welcome there.

"Hey, Rusty, how's it goin'? I guess you thought I was never going to get out here to see you. I've been pretty busy lately."

"I'm not worried about you, Ron. I know you've got more to do than drop everything when I call."

"Steve said you had found a house you thought I might be interested in."

"Yeah." Rusty was nodding. "It's a two-bedroom house on Hurricane Creek Road. My in-laws live on that road farther down toward the lake. I think Johnny Riddle owns the house."

"Sounds like something I'd like to take a look at. How much land is with it?"

"Six acres. If you want to, we can ride out there and look at it now."

"Hey, that would be great."

After driving to the house, Ron really liked what he saw. He drove back to the store, and dialed Linda.

"Hey, hon, can you meet me out here at Rusty's store? I looked at that house. I'd like for you to see it."

"Okay. See you in a few minutes."

It wasn't long before they were moving to the cute little house on Hurricane Creek. Steve and his wife took the apartment at the jail. The Cunninghams felt safe. Life went on.

One evening while the move was in process, the phone at the sheriff's office rang.

"Ron, it's for you. The guy from Mobile."

"Hey, Sheriff! I've got good news and bad news for you. Which do you want first?"

"Good news."

"We located Price and it will cost a case of Jack Daniel."

"Okay…"

The wily investigator had been with the department in Mobile long enough to know all the ins and outs. He had a menagerie of informants. He had contacted a well-known cab driver in town and told him about the Jack Daniel reward. The cab driver then informed the investigator that he had picked Price up and dropped him at a local bar. The investigator arrived at the bar and located the subject. Next came the bad news: Price had resisted arrest and pulled a gun, causing a shoot-out to ensue. Price had been shot, but was taken into custody and hospitalized. Due to the severity of his injuries, he could not be moved. The officer advised Ron that when Price's condition was sufficiently improved, he would have to go through the extradition process to get him back to Tennessee.

"Don't worry, man. I'll get a "Fugitive from Justice" warrant and when he is able, I'll help you get him back to Tennessee."

"Thanks, man."

It was about a month before Ron received another call from the D.A.s office in Chattanooga.

"James' attorney has petitioned the court to separate his case from that of the Rivers' and wants a court date set to hear that petition."

"Do I need to be there?"

"No. Not unless you want to. I'll call you and let you know the judge's decision."

It seemed an eternity before the call finally came.

"Ron, this is Investigator Joe Smithson in Mobile."

"What's up?"

"You can come on down and pick up Price. The extradition process is completed."

"Great. See you in a couple days."

By the time the sheriff arrived in Mobile he was mentally exhausted. He had driven the arduous journey through Birmingham, around all of the confusing detours caused by the extensive road repairs, to Montgomery, where he had checked into a motel, called home and conked out for the night. At the crack of dawn on Wednesday morning he had headed south with one goal in mind.

The city limit of Mobile was a welcome sight. Ron scanned the map and tried to keep his eyes on the road while he located the station.

"Hey, I'm Ron Cunningham from Tennessee. I'm here to pick up a prisoner—Barry Price. Is Investigator Smithson around?"

"Yeah. He's been expecting you. I'll call him."

"Hi, Ron, Joe. Sorry, but I'm afraid I've got some more bad news for you."

Ron sighed deeply. "What this time?"

"Price escaped. Don't know where he is!"

"Escaped?! What the heck happened?"

"We've got to enter him in the NCIC as a fugitive."

"Right. Let's get it done."

"I brought the case of Jack Daniel's. I'll leave it with you for the taxi driver, but I need my man. That's the deal!"

"You know I'll do my best."

Redd's Grocery crew in front of store

Left to right, Sammy Johnson,

Angelica Lightfoot, Bobbie Redd,

And Doug Harold Young

Photo: Stan St. Clair

CHAPTER ELEVEN

"Sheriff, this is District Attorney Gary Gerbitz in Hamilton County. The judge denied Earl James' petition to separate the cases."

"Doesn't surprise me. I'm glad to hear it."

"Hey, when are we going to get together for the tour of Jack Daniel's and the lunch at Bobo's Boarding House?"

"Don't worry, Gary. I haven't forgotten it. The tours are no problem, but I'll set the lunch up and give you a call."

It was April, 1979. Flowers dusted the landscape, and Moore County was dressed in her most glorious and flowing gown.

More than a quarter of a million folks had visited Lynchburg each year, and the trend continues to this day. For many of them it has been a pilgrimage to see the famous distillery where Jack Daniel's Whisky had been proudly produced for more than a century and a half.

Miss Mary Bobo's began as a traveler's hotel in 1867, and quickly became the convenient locale for Jack Daniel's employees and visitors alike to gather for a tasty noonday meal. Miss Mary would continue to operate her vogue boarding house until her death in 1983, only one month shy of her 102nd birthday.

Miss Mary Bobo's Boarding House Restaurant still stands today, welcoming countless tourists and locals for Southern home-cooked lunches.

The following day Ron made the call. The proprietor was the great-grandniece of Jack Daniel, himself, Lynne Tolley.

"Hey, Lynne, this is Ron Cunningham. I need to set up a lunch for a group."

"Now, Sheriff, you know that whenever you want it, you've got it!"

"Well, I've got to go back to Chattanooga for court with Rivers and James this summer. Let's set this for the first Monday in August. That way I hope we can get everybody notified properly."

"Sounds great, Sheriff, I've got you down. How many will be in your party?"

"Well, if we get everybody, there should be eighteen. They're coming from Chattanooga, but some of the fellas are from Michigan."

"See you then, Ron."

Three weeks had seemed to fly by and Ron had not heard from Smithson in Mobile. He began to wonder if he had wasted a perfectly good case of Jack Daniel.

"Sheriff, there's a guy on the phone from Florida!" Steve frowned as he handed Ron the phone.

"Ron Cunningham, may I help you?"

"Yeah, Sheriff. This is Captain Morris Jordan in Fort Lauderdale. I've got a Barry Price in custody. I believe you have dibs on him."

Ron's face lit up. "Yeah! That's good news."

"But there's more. Not so good, I'm afraid. He resisted arrest and was injured in a fight with one of our officers. He's in the hospital under guard."

"That seems to be a pattern with him."

"As soon as he is released and goes through the extradition process we will notify you and you can come and transport him back to Tennessee."

Ron hung up and dialed D.A. Gary Girbitz to make sure about the next court date.

"Well, Ron. It will be late summer because the defense attorney filed a motion to suppress evidence."

"Well, I set up the Jack Daniel's tour and the lunch at Miss Mary Bobo's for the first Monday in August."

"That'll be fine. I look forward to it."

On the 5th of June, Ron got another call from Fort Lauderdale. Price was finally ready for extradition.

Early the next morning the eager sheriff once again bid his family adieu and drove to BNA to catch the first flight out for South Florida.

As the Boeing 747 taxied down the runway at Fort Lauderdale-Hollywood Airport, the local investigators and SWAT team members stared out the glass panels eagerly awaiting his advent.

Ron was almost amused, but not laughing. Barry Price was not only handcuffed, but shackled by ankle cuffs which were connected to a belly chain. No one was taking any chances of another escape attempt.

Ron at once realized the severity of his problem here. Not only could Price not board a plane in this apparatus, but the sheriff would not even be permitted to take a firearm on board. He must establish some boundaries of respect with his prisoner.

"Take off the cuffs and chains," Ron said calmly.

"When we do that," said Morris, "he's gonna run!"

"Take them off!" Ron repeated emphatically.

Morris shook his head, and complied. The country sheriff could feel every eye upon him.

Ron ambled up to Price and stared deep into his blazing eyes, his finger pointing across the runway.

"Okay, Price, now's your chance. Take off running as fast as you can!" As he was speaking, the sheriff removed the .357 Magnum from its holster which he had retrieved from his baggage and pointed it at Price's forehead. "If you can make it to the end of the runway before I bring you down, you're a free man!"

Price turned and looked at the end of the runway, then back at the sheriff. "You serious?" he managed.

"Absolutely! I'd just as soon carry you back in a pine box. Less trouble that way. And it would save me from fighting you in court, too."

"You really mean it, don't you, Sheriff?"

"I do."

"Okay, then, I won't give you any trouble."

The sheriff and his prisoner boarded their flight back to Nashville and got settled.

"What would you gentlemen like to drink?"

Ron looked up into the eyes of an attractive slender flight attendant. "What ya want, Price?'

"Well, what I really want is a Jack and Coke, but I know you won't let me have it."

Ron smiled slightly. "You can have anything you want till we get back to the jail."

"Give it to him. Make mine just Coke."

In Atlanta there was a three hour layover, in which they were able to have steaks at a restaurant. Not only did Ron permit Price two Jack Daniel's and Coke, but a knife to cut his steak.

"Sheriff, no one has ever treated me this nice before." Tears were in the corners of Barry Price's eyes.

"I appreciate you saying that. You treat me the way I want to be treated, and I will treat you the same. That's the Golden Rule. I will continue to treat you well as long as you behave yourself."

"Don't worry. I won't give you any more trouble."

The remainder of the trip back to Lynchburg went off without a hitch.

Two weeks had passed. Price had been a model prisoner.

"Barry, I will make you a trustee if you will give me your word that you won't try anything stupid."

"Don't worry, Sheriff. Haven't I been good?"

"Yeah, so far." Ron unlocked the cell. "You have to stay with me at all times."

"You got it."

Price was a well-mannered trustee, went through the court process, and was in route to Nashville to serve his time in the Federal Penitentiary. On the way, he started a fight with the guards who were transporting him and escaped again.

CHAPTER TWELVE

"Sheriff, Dottie Thomas' mother is on the phone for you. Says she's got information on Davy."

"Thanks, Steve." Ron rolled his eyes. *She has it in for him. This better be legit.* "Ron Cunningham, may I help you?"

"Yeah, Sheriff. This is Sally Jarrett, Davy Thomas' mother in law."

"Sure. I know who you are."

"Dottie called me, collect, mind you. I started not to take the call, but I thought somethin' might be wrong. Like she might be hurt or somethin'. Ever since she left with that sorry man of hers I've been worried about her. She wouldn't tell me where they are, but she said she was workin' at a motel, and Davy was workin' next door at a service station doin' mechanic work. 'Bout all he's good for."

"The boy is a good mechanic. I tell you what, when you get the phone bill, bring it by my office and we'll run the number. I appreciate you calling."

Davy Thomas was doing state time on a burglary charge, and had been a trustee, and a very hard worker. Ron felt that he just needed someone to really care and give him some guidance. Dottie had visited him several times, so Ron had no reason to suspect anything when she had come by that day that she and Davy has vanished. It had been months and there had been no leads.

When the phone bill came, Sally brought it in, and Ron saw that it was a Detroit number. He called the Detroit Police Department and spoke with an investigator who traced it to a phone booth at the motel where Dottie Thomas was employed.

Ron sent pictures of Davy and Dottie to the investigator in Detroit and he called and verified that the couple was still living and working there.

"I'm coming up to get Thomas. Have someone keep an eye on them till I get there."

"Will do, Sheriff. See you in a day or so."

When Ron arrived at the police station the investigator accompanied him to apprehend the fugitive.

"Hi, I'm Sheriff Ron Cunningham from Moore County, Tennessee. I need to speak with one of your employees, Davy Thomas."

"You're not going to like this, Sheriff, but your man, Davy, and his wife found out you were coming for him, so they packed up and left this morning."

Ron let out a quick sigh of disgust. "Did he say where they were headed?"

"Oh, sure. Canada."

"There are just two places you can get into Canada from here," the officer said with resolve in his tone. "One's a tunnel, the other's a bridge."

The detective grabbed his mike and radioed the station. "This is Captain Jed Jacobs. Have a two-man team go to the Detroit-Windsor Tunnel. Sheriff Cunningham and I are en route to Ambassador Bridge. Put out an APB on David Thomas, aka Davy Thomas and his wife, Dorothy Ann Jarrett Thomas, aka Dottie. They're driving a two-door blue 1970 Ford Fairlane, Tennessee license plate number 954-NLT. Pictures on file."

"Roger, copy,"

"What the heck? This traffic is backed up something fierce." Jacobs said.

"But look! I think that's them just ahead of us."

"By golly, I think you're right, Cunningham. But they're only about three cars from the bridge gate! And there are quite a few vehicles between us. We don't have a snowball's chance in hell of catching them before they get across!"

"I can't accept that. Where there's a will there's a way."

Ron put his cruiser in park and bolted onto the pavement. By the time he reached the suspect's vehicle, it was last in line before the gate where passports are checked! The driver's window was open, so Ron reached inside and shoved the gearshift into park, then jerked the door open and grabbed Thomas, slamming him to the ground and placing the cuffs on his wrists.

Jacobs had followed, but the entire ordeal was over before he reached the scene.

"What do you want done with the suspect's vehicle?" Jacobs asked, still in a state of disbelief at what had just unfolded before him.

"Have it towed."

"Can his wife just drive it back?"

"No. Cuff her. Have it towed in."

Both waived extradition and were placed in the back of Ron's cruiser for their return trip to Tennessee.

Only restroom breaks were allowed going back and fast food was consumed in the car.

New charges were filed on both suspects; both were convicted and sent to the state penitentiary in Nashville to serve their time.

CHAPTER THIRTEEN

During his trying ordeal with Davy and Dottie Thomas, Ron had been crossing off the days on his calendar, anxiously awaiting the court date so justice could be served in his own case. Finally it was August sixth—the first Monday and time for the tour of Jack Daniel's.

There were a total of sixteen who were subpoenaed for the Grand Jury hearing as witnesses. These included, besides prosecutor/victim Sheriff Ron Cunningham, eight law enforcement officers of varying status and branches of service—state, local and federal. They also called the three undercover agents and seven other witnesses which were not directly involved in the sting.

These witnesses involved were: Lacy "Moon" Brown, Lapeer County, Michigan Sheriff's Department; Robert "Phil" McCarty, Port

Huron, Michigan Police Department; Joseph Vince, ATF (Federal Bureau of Tobacco, Firearms and Explosives) Agent, Flint, Michigan; Louis Ilano, Flint, Michigan Police Department; Danny Wix, TBI Agent, Manchester, Tennessee; Jerry W. Eubanks, TBI Agent, Fayetteville, Tennessee; Steve Wortham, TBI Agent, Nashville, Tennessee; Julian Bomar, ATF Agent, Nashville, Tennessee.

Additional witnesses subpoenaed were TBI Agents Joe Helton and James Parrott; ATF Agents Colvin Little, Winston Davidson, Bob Richards and John Franklin of Chattanooga, and Walter Rangenburg of Detroit, Michigan.

Along with the D.A. and second chair, there were eighteen who showed up for the tour and lunch at Miss Mary Bobo's.

The tour began at 10:00 AM and their tour guide was William Grogan, who was married to the former Freda Cunningham, a second cousin of the sheriff. William was very professional, informative, witty and jovial.

The tour itself lasted about two hours. The group covered roughly nine acres on foot after a brief introduction accompanied by a film. This jaunt took them in and out of warehouses with about eighteen different stops. The first of these was at the rick yard where they burn sugar maple wood, after splashing it with a bit of their own 135 proof whisky, to produce charcoal which is used to aid in the mellowing process.

Then, the group stopped at the limestone cave spring from which the water originates for the production of Jack Daniel's unique whisky. Grogan explained the fact that this water is so cool, pure and iron-free that it is used for no other purpose. The source from which this spring flows remains unknown to this day.

Next, the tour visited Mr. Daniel's personal office, which is located in the only remaining original building on the premises. They were shown the old rusty safe which is said to have led to Mr. Daniel's death. The story goes that when he was unable to open it one morning, he became frustrated and kicked it, causing a terrible infection to develop on his foot, which went untreated and eventually caused his demise.

The closest they came to actually sampling the product was during the presentation on the fermenting process.

Distilling the whiskey combines corn, rye and barley along with the pure spring water to create what is known as "mash". It is actually called "sour mash" as it is left to bubble and age gracefully.

After that, they were able to witness the mellowing process as the mixture slowly dripped through ten feet of charcoal.

William then invited the group to stand close to the giant tank while he rapidly opened and closed the lid. While doing so he encouraged them to breathe deeply, inhaling the pungent vapors. "Now," he said with a simper, "you can taste the richness of the whiskey!"

Finally, they were able to see a barrel filling up and the storage warehouse for the multitude of barrels of famous Jack Daniel's 135 proof whiskey.

They ended their fascinating tour back at the visitor's center and were treated to all the Jack Daniel's lemonade they wanted.

Then they were off to Miss Mary Bobo's for a scrumptious Southern lunch.

When Miss Mary had begun her boarding house in 1908, she was but a youthful spinster. The building then housed the historic Salmon Hotel, of which she assumed ownership. As a traveler's rest, it had been constructed over a spring.

The building is a charming, white-painted Federal-style with giant maple trees gracing the front lawn. A spacious porch supports swings and wooden chairs in which guests may lounge before or after their meal. There was also a lovely assortment of ferns and flowers. Meals are only served on Mondays between 11:00 AM and 1:00 PM, and sixty-five persons are accommodated at each setting.

Lynne Tolley had asked Ron to have the group there half an hour early in order to be seated at the proper time.

The ringing of the dinner bell let Ron know that it was time for them to enter their assigned dining area.

"Follow me," said their hostess, a lovely local lady, "Y'all will be eating in the basement. That way you'll gain the most authentic atmosphere of the original restaurant. Even the kitchen was there to begin with."

The group descended the quaint wooden staircase and the sheriff pointed out to his guests the classy brick floors.

Moon couldn't help notice the enchanting spring which lay beneath them. He felt right at home, as he loved natural springs. He longed to join his parents in rural North Carolina, and soon he would.

"This casserole is unreal!" McCarty said.

"For sure, Ron agreed. And the apples are cooked with Jack in them!"

"No wonder they're so tasty. Thanks for bringing us here," D. A. Gerbitz said. You know what's good around here."

"Thanks, man." Ron smiled and nodded.

After a satisfying meal, topped off with pumpkin chess square cake, with cream cheese icing and smothered in crushed pecans, served by bouncy Motlow students, the Grand Jury witness team was ready to go. They separated late with full stomachs and a heart full of grand memories, looking forward with mixed emotions to meeting again on the day of the trial.

Miss Mary Bobo's Boarding House

and Restaurant

Photo, Rhonda St. Clair

CHAPTER FOURTEEN

Ron was soon informed that the trial had once again been postponed due to motions pending.

Disappointed yet determined, he was again forced to set his hopes on a future trial date and focus on the job at hand. As usual, there was no shortage of work for the sheriff.

One especially trying case was that of Greg Horton.

Late one afternoon as Ron was preparing to call it a day, an elderly lady in obvious disarray came crashing through the front door of the jail.

"Sheriff!" she puffed, "I was kidnapped by your escaped prisoner, Greg Horton, and I've been through torment! You've got to get that fella, I was held prisoner and…"

"Ma'am, sit down here and give me a complete statement. Let me get a form here."

"Yes sir. I've just been through so much I don't know where to start."

"Start at the beginning."

"Well, in the middle of the night, while I was sound asleep...I didn't even hear nothin'; I felt this hand over my mouth. Then this rough voice says, 'You make a sound and I'll stab you to death!' He had a pair of scissors pushin' 'em against my side. I thought I was a goner! He made me give him my car keys and he took me out while I was still in my nightgown. He drove me through Tullahoma all the way to the Red Food Store over in Decherd. Then he took me behind the store and took them scissors and cut off my pocketbook straps and tied me up, and tied a rag around my mouth. He took my car and left. I got no idea where he went, but he came back in a while and untied me and made me go in the store and cash my Social Security check and give him the money.

"Then he drove me to Nashville to the Greyhound bus station. He made me buy him a ticket to Florida by writing a check. He gave me back my keys and I made a bee-line for your office. I got here as fast as I could."

"Well, that bus to Florida goes right through Tullahoma, and with the stops it has on the way, I think I can beat it there! Go on home and get some rest."

Greg Horton was originally being held on charges of sexual abuse of a minor, and other crimes. When the bus arrived it was no trouble to apprehend the escapee. Now he would face a whole battery of new charges. Like kidnapping, robbery and escape.

While awaiting trial, he squeezed his slender frame through the bars at the food entrance during the night and sneaked downstairs and made 900 number calls for phone sex, then silently returned to his cell. This routine continued over a period of months. When the phone bills showed up and the prisoners were questioned, another inmate "ratted" on Horton.

After interrogation by the sheriff, Horton admitted to the calls and was subsequently charged with this offence as well.

Early the following morning, Horton was missing. Ron was frowning as he answered the phone.

"Sheriff, this is Bob Burton out near Mulberry. Somebody stole one of my horses this morning. When I went to feed them I saw that one was missing, and a Western style saddle I bought from the co-op and a bridle."

"We've got a prisoner missing. It's a sure bet he's not coming this way. I'm betting he headed for Fayetteville."

Ron called the Lincoln County Sheriff's Department and later got a call that a man fitting Horton's description had sold a horse at the stock barn that day and caught a cab to the airport in Huntsville, Alabama.

Ron called the airport and was told that Horton's flight had a four-hour layover in Atlanta. After calling the Metro Atlanta PD and security at Hartsfield International Airport, Ron got in his cruiser and with the blue lights and siren screaming headed for the Interstate toward Atlanta.

When Horton re-boarded for takeoff, Ron was waiting, along with the local authorities. After being apprehended, Horton waived extradition proceedings and was returned to Lynchburg by the sheriff and transferred to the state pen in Nashville, where he remained incarcerated until his court date. After his trial and conviction in Moore County he was returned to Nashville to serve his time.

The Tullahoma News had run the headline, "Prisoner escapes, steals horse and rides off into the sunset".

Ron would later learn that after his term in Nashville was served, Horton ended up getting into more trouble in Texas. There, while serving time in the state prison, he stabbed another inmate to death, and eventually was killed himself in the same senseless fashion.

But for now Ron had again made certain that justice continued to prevail—for others. Somehow, however, it seemed to elude Rivers and James.

CHAPTER FIFTEEN

Ron had requested a status report from the court in Hamilton County on his case. The next morning after Horton was sent to Nashville he opened the envelope and looked down at the exasperating chain of delays in the case against his accused would-be killers.

On April 25th Jerry Simmons had filed a motion to withdraw as Nona Rivers' attorney. On June 8th James Henry had filed a motion for continuance on behalf of John McCord, James' attorney, due to illness. Now another motion had been filed for a Bill of Particulars. 1979 was fast slipping away, and he felt helpless in his fervent desire to reach closure. What else could happen?

Lewis McGee and Bobbie Redd's dad, Clifton Hall, worked for the Moore County Highway Department. That warm early September morning they were delivering a load of gravel to Don Ellis' home near Redd's Grocery.

A suspicious vehicle with two young men was driving back and forth along the rural roads every morning between 7:00 and 8:00 o'clock. While the men were delivering the gravel, the vehicle kept passing the Ellis' home, and Lewis McGee wrote down the tag number with his finger in the dust. That morning the car had stopped at Redd's and the driver had bought $2.00 worth of gas. Bobbie went out to pump the gas.

"Can you tell me where Ridgeville Road is?" the driver asked.

"Right there," Bobbie Redd answered, pointing to the nearby intersection.

"Thanks," came the smug answer.

Rusty and Bobbie's daughter, Judy Young, was in the store eyeing the car.

"That car has turned around in my driveway several times. Those fellas are up to no good," she told her mother when she returned.

"I'm calling the sheriff.

"Hey, Ron. This is Bobbie Redd. We just had a car stop here and get a couple of dollars worth of gas which has been scoping out the neighborhood. They headed out onto Ridgeville Road. I think you need to check it out."

"Thanks, Bobbie. I'll be right there."

"What's that all about?" TBI Agent Larry Wallace asked.

"Suspicious vehicle report. Might be a good thing you're here. Want to go with me?"

"Sure, why not."

The car had pulled into Houston Tankersly's driveway, backed up to the den door, and dragged out a cedar chest, and other small personal items and furniture, and were beginning to load them in the car.

McGee had blocked the driveway with the gravel truck. When Ron and Wallace arrived, the passenger, a nervous young man with cross-eyes, ran through the field and into the woods, but the driver had remained in the car, cutting through the yard, averting the roadblock. He was nowhere to be seen.

The house had been ransacked and was a total mess. Piles of personal items, including the cedar chest, were stacked at the back door. Houston Tankersly was from an old money family, and viewed as a great potential for a hit.

Lewis McGee gave Ron the tag number.

"Thanks, man. I really appreciate your help."

Ron first radioed in the tag number, and found that it was registered to Oren Prince of Shelbyville. Then he and Wallace returned to Redd's, and related what had happened.

Bobbie then called Mrs. Tankersly at Wilson's Sporting Goods in Tullahoma where she was working. Houston worked at AEDC and was difficult to contact.

"Corrine, this is Bobbie at the store. Was anyone supposed to be at your house today?"

"No, why?'

"Someone just broke into you folk's house and ransacked it. Thank God, Ron got here in time to save most everything."

"My goodness! Thank you for calling, Bobbie. Do you have any idea who it was?"

"Ron has the tag number of the vehicle. He found out who it belongs to. I'm sure he'll be in touch."

In the meantime, Prince was cruising around Hurricane Creek Road honking his horn, frantically searching for his accomplice.

"Bobbie, how about fixing me a bologna and cheese sandwich? We might as well settle down a while and let this guy go home."

"Sure, Ron," Bobbie said. "I know how you like it. You want some chips, too?"

"Sure, and I'll get me a root beer."

"Sounds good to me." Wallace ordered, and they all sat around a while and visited with the Redds and their customers, enjoying being in out of the heat.

"Let's go to Shelbyville, shall we?"

"Sounds like a winner." Larry Wallace smiled and they headed out.

Upon arriving at Shelbyville they obtained a search warrant from the Bedford County authorities, drove to the Prince home, and knocked.

"Oren Prince, I'm Sheriff Ron Cunningham of Moore County, and this is Agent Larry Wallace with the TBI. We have a warrant to search your home."

"What are you guys lookin' for?"

"We have reason to believe that your car was used in a home break in down in Moore County this morning."

"Come on in. You won't find anything here."

After a thorough search of the premises, the officers were about to leave, when Ron looked under Prince's bed and noticed a large rug.

"Help me here, Larry. There's something strange about this."

The two moved the bed and pulled the rug back, revealing a trap door which led to stairs descending to a hidden basement. In that basement were the belongings removed from the Tankersly home, along with scores of other items which fit the description of missing property from a string of other recent robberies around Middle Tennessee.

"Oren Prince, you're under arrest for the break in and burglary of the home of Houston Tankersly in Moore County. You may remain silent. Anything you say can and will be used against you in a court of law. You are entitled to an attorney. If you cannot afford one, one will be appointed for you by the court."

As a result of Prince's arrest, all of the Tankersly's property was recovered, and several other crimes were solved.

Circuit Court Judge Robert Parks heard the case. The DA was Jack Bomar, and Ron Wilson was his assistant.

Prince stated that he had purchased a number of the items from two young men, one of which turned out to be the person who had fled from the Tankersley property. Both were arrested and convicted of their involvement in these incidents.

Prince was found guilty and served time in the state penitentiary.

Larry Wallace was appointed Director of the Tennessee Bureau of Investigation in 1992 by then Governor, Ned McWhorter, and served until 2003 under Governors Don Sunquist and Phil Bredesen. He was twice elected Sheriff of

McMinn County, and has served as Colonel and Commanding Officer of the Tennessee Highway Patrol, and Deputy Commissioner of the Tennessee Department of Safety. He currently serves as the Vice President of External Affairs for Tennessee Wesleyan College.

Former TBI Director, Larry Wallace*

CHAPTER SIXTEEN

Fall was finally settling in on beautiful Moore County. Late one afternoon Ron was sitting alone in his office relaxing, sipping on a root beer. The air was noticeably a bit cool, but the change was welcome after a long, scorching summer.

Ron was so relaxed that the ringing of the phone jolted him back to reality.

"Moore County Sheriff's Office, Sheriff Cunningham, may I help you?"

"Ron, this is Laura Brown, Moon's wife. We've never met, but I've heard a lot about you, how you guy's worked together and all.

"We've moved to Troy, North Carolina and bought about three hundred acres over here. It's way out in the middle of nowhere..." Laura's soft voice trailed.

"That's great, but you sound like something's wrong. What seems to be the trouble?" Ron asked.

"Well, these people have been driving by harassing him. Shooting at the house, cursing at him and the kids. He's called the local sheriff's office and they came out to our place and talked to him. But they said there's nothing they can do!

"I was just wondering if you had a few days, if you could come up here and spend some time with him. I believe it would really make him feel better."

"Sure," said Ron, "I have a little time off anyhow. It's been kinda hectic around here. Let me speak with him a minute, if you don't mind."

Laura held the phone away from her mouth and called Moon. "Lacy, Ron wants to talk to you."

"Hey, brother, how's it going?" Moon was grinning as he talked.

"Oh, pretty good," Ron said. "How's it with you?"

"A little rough right now. You think you can get away for a few days?"

"You bet, I'm looking forward to seeing you again. Give me a couple of days to put some loose ends together and I'll be on my way! I'll give you a ring when I leave."

"Okay," said Moon. "I'll see you in a few."

After two days Ron made the call and got directions to the Brown's home.

The road seemed endless to Troy, North Carolina, and at the end of a full day's drive and a fruitless search for the house, dusk was falling. Ron stopped and called to make sure where he was going.

"Hey, buddy, I've been up and down this road a half a dozen times trying to locate your place."

"It *is* hard to find," Moon said, "it's up on a hill. I'll turn the porch light on and have the kids stand out on the side of the hill wearing white T- shirts."

Moon's plan worked. Not only were the kids wearing white T-shirts, they were yelling, and the porch light was blinking off and on! But the narrow drive was still difficult to see.

The Brown's home was an older farm house positioned a good distance off of a country gravel road far back in the Carolina hills. Soft gray smoke was curling from the dull-red-brick chimney. A chilling breeze was puffing in, announcing the advent of an eminent winter.

After being properly introduced to Moon's wife and family, Mother Nature came knocking on Ron's door.

"I hate to ask so soon, but I've been on the road, and have to go. Could you please tell me where your rest room is?"

"Uh...we don't have indoor plumbing." Moon said apologetically, "Just go through the kitchen out the back door, and follow the path across the road."

The mere trip through the kitchen was an adventure of its own — it was like walking back through time. There sat an old wood cook stove with a pan of water on one eye, and an antique coffeepot on another. Following a path to an outside toilet was another travel through time.

After returning to the living room and backing up to a wood heater to knock off the chill, Ron was again directed to the pan of water on the cook stove in the kitchen where he could "freshen up", and was handed a hot cup of newly-brewed java from the old percolator.

Moon, his family, Ron and a mother dog, which was in cardboard box behind the stove with her pups, shared their companionship and conversation until the wee hours before finally falling asleep.

The next morning was Sunday. Ron awoke late to the smell of coffee and bacon. And once again, his body was telling him to head out the path he had taken the night before.

The walk to the outhouse in the cold brought back old memories for the sheriff. But this trip would put him in a unique position which he would never forget. This memory always brings him laughter every time it crosses his mind.

The latrine was a two-seater. But the kicker was the fact that it had no door. Thus, no privacy. While seated on the toilet, a woman drove by in a station wagon filled with young children. They were pointing, laughing and waving. The woman driver was even waving. Ron felt like ducking out of sight, but there was nowhere to go, and nothing to do but wave back. Ron's pale face turned sanguine.

Back in the house he enjoyed a hale and hearty breakfast of bacon, eggs, gravy and biscuits topped off with at least a couple of cups of fresh, tasty coffee. But who was counting. But, of course, he had to share his experience of his cold trip to the john, and the event which heated up his blood pressure.

Moon, Ron and the kids spent the rest of the day wandering through the hills, following the plentiful cool streams which flowed through the beautiful landscape of his place, panning for gold. They were pleased to find a few shiny nuggets, and some dust which they removed with an eye dropper from the inside ridges of the pans.

To pan for gold, they dipped the pans into the stream and swished the water around, then poured it back into the stream. Next, the eye dropper was partially filled with water and used to suck the dust out of the pan. Then the contents of the eye dropper were squeezed into a small vial filled with water. The dust would sink to the bottom of the vial. This process was continued until the vial was filled with dust. It took Ron all day to fill his vial. The small nuggets were found by lifting up rocks from the black-looking silt.

By the time they got back to the house it was late afternoon, and everyone was treated to a hot supper of roast beef, potatoes, fried okra, pinto beans, corn, collard greens, tomatoes, corn bread and ice tea. For dessert there was mouth-watering banana pudding!

Ron had another Troy, North Carolina hills surprise waiting for him after this scrumptious meal. Moon and his boys grabbed some clean towels and one for their guest.

"Come on," Moon called out. "Let's go take a bath!"

They all trooped out the back door, down the path to the gravel road, then to the highway, and across to an old rock quarry.

"This place is fed by several cold springs which flow into here year-round. The water's always cold in this quarry. Bet you can't find the bottom!"

"Bet I don't try!" Ron returned.

"This is the way we do it," Moon said with a grin as he and the boys stripped off their clothes.

"Last one in's a rotten egg!" one of the boys screamed as he wrapped his arms around his knees and hit the water with a thud. One by one they all followed suit.

Again Ron was a victim of circumstances. The frigid water sent chills up and down Ron's spine, but soon he adjusted. They all climbed out and soaped down their bodies, then got back in and rinsed off. Finally they climbed out again, toweled off and dressed. Ron left as refreshed as if he had just bathed in the Ganges.

When they got back to the house Ron was shivering and hugging the toasty stove.

Once again that evening everyone sat around talking. This time, reminiscing about the adventures of that bodacious day—one none of them would ever forget—long into the night. But tonight Ron would sleep by the stove with the mama dog and her pups.

Sometime early the next morning Ron awoke to the whimpering of the little ones and a stove void of heat. Mama fed her pups and Ron fed the stove. Everyone was then able to drift back to dreamland.

After another huge breakfast of bacon, eggs, gravy, biscuits and coffee, Ron said his good-byes and headed back to the familiar land of Lynchburg and Moore County.

On the road home the sheriff thanked God for his friends, his family and the tension-free few days which he had been blessed to spend with his dear friend, Moon.

The two-seater at Moon's

Photo property of Ron Cunningham

CHAPTER SEVENTEEN

The winter was a little less hectic. But even during Christmas Ron's mind was on getting the case heard and justice served.

Ron knew that there were any number of people who had no use for him and wouldn't think twice about finding a way to get even.

Early the next year it was time for a little break. Linda had family in Lima, Ohio, and they would travel up for a short visit.

In Cincinnati, Ron pulled off for gas at a station with an adjoining restaurant, and noticed a group of motorcycles parked around the building. A rough-looking female attendant came out and filled up Ron's tank. She kept glancing down at his tag with the sheriff department logo. Ron was glancing in his rear-view mirror.

The attendant motioned to one of the motorcyclists who was about to climb on his bike.

As the man approached his breath was freezing and floating through the coldness of the city. Ron could barely make out the fact that the attendant was talking to him about his Moore County tag.

Before he could pay for the gas, the cyclist was at his door.

"Hey, dude, are you with the Moore County, Tennessee Sheriff Department?"

"Yeah, I am."

"You look familiar, man. I was down there a few years ago and I was locked up by some freakin' big fig that looked like you. Now you wouldn't know anything about that, would you?"

"Yes, I would," Ron said sternly. "That was me. And I'd do the same again if I needed to." Ron was reaching under his seat as he spoke.

"You were on your turf then, dog. Now you're on mine!"

Ron slowly laid his .357 Magnum on the dash. "Maybe so. I was nice to you then, but I don't have to be Mr. Nice Guy any more. I've got my little baby here with me."

Linda sat still and put her right index finger over her mouth, motioning for the girls to be quiet.

"Well, I can show up out of nowhere when you are least expecting me. This thing's not over, you know."

"You don't have to look for me. I'm on my way to Lima to visit family." Ron was scribbling on a card. "Here's where I'll be. My friend here and I will be waiting for you." Ron patted his .357 and grinned.

The trip was made without further ado. Once again he had bitten the bullet.

Barry Price had been a fugitive for a year now. After Ron got home, Barry called his office.

"Sheriff, I'm tired of running. I want to turn myself in."

"Why are you calling me?" Ron asked.

"I don't want to turn myself in to anyone but you."

"Come on down. I'll be glad to see that you are treated fairly."

And so the saga of Barry Price came to a fitting conclusion. Ron personally transported him to

Nashville with no further incident where he served his sentence.

Ron walked in early one February morning and found Steve already on the phone.

"Sheriff, it's for you," he said, handing off the big black phone.

"Ron Cunningham, here, may I help you?"

"Sheriff, this is District Attorney Gary Gerbitz in Hamilton County again. We've finally got a court date that I believe will stick."

"Great! When is it?"

"Two months away. Wednesday, April 16th."

"I'll be there with bells on."

CHAPTER EIGHTEEN

Wednesday morning, 16 April 1980 finally arrived. Well over a year had expired since the arrest of Rivers and James. As Ron sat on the hard bench in the in Hamilton County Courthouse in downtown Chattanooga awaiting the opening of the Second Division of Criminal Court of the Sixth Judicial District, he shut out the din of the chatting around him. His mind went to his beloved Moore County. To Ron, she was like a beautiful lady with whom he had fallen deeply in love from his earliest youth. His stint in the service of the country had been a great adventure, and had served as a schoolmaster toward the more specific aid to his county. He had longed to embrace her and drink in the sensual satisfaction which he only could experience in her presence. Moore County was Love personified. Her lush green hillsides and the perfume of the flowers in springtime resonated in his heart like nowhere else. Even in the chill of winter there seemed to remain an unexplained thrill. Ron had felt peace in his return which had been threatened and violated by the macabre conspiracy which had almost ripped his life away. The hurt which it had caused his family and the threat to their future could never be justified. Nevertheless, he longed for some semblance of justice to emerge from it.

Earl James was whispering to his attorney, John McCord. The words were too undefined for Ron to decipher. Attorney Hank Mount was showing a paper to Clint Rivers.

The two had been federally indicted in March on two counts in relation to Ron's case: conspiracy to take human life and solicitation of first degree murder.

The judge entered and calm gradually swept over the sullen room. "All rise. Sixth Judicial Court is now in session, the honorable Judge Joseph Solano presiding. You may be seated. Court is now in session."

Judge Solano rapped the gavel on the bench and cleared his throat. "The first case today is the state versus Parsons..."

Ron's mind now focused on justice. A smile came across his face. Only a few days ago a case very near and dear to his heart had finally been settled. He could not have been happier for his friend.

Late on Friday night, August 19th, 1977, Ron, who was attending a church service in Winchester, received a call to respond to a serious single car auto accident on Ledford Mill Road. Arriving first on the scene, even before State Trooper Randy Pierce, he attempted to gain entrance to the white two-door sedan, and found the doors jammed. The scene inside was ominous. Three teenagers in the car were obviously in immediate danger of death, if not dead already. Shortly, the EMTs arrived. Taking off his jacket, Ron used it to protect his hands while breaking out the right rear window to remove the passengers from the back seat while the techs took out the front passengers. It was immediately obvious that front-seat passenger, eighteen-year-old Becky Lynn Nokes, was not breathing, and had no pulse. Back-seat passenger, seventeen-year-old Keith Anspach was wedged between the front passenger seat and the bottom of the rear seat, his legs extending over his head from the back. As Ron lifted Keith from the mangled wreckage, he was making no movement. "That one's dead, too." The EMT was emphatic in his assessment.

"Just a minute! He's gurgling. He's alive!" Ron exclaimed. "Get him on some oxygen!"

The group of teens had just left an outing at the Mill attended primarily by a group of their peers who had all graduated that spring from Tullahoma High School.

As the car, driven by eighteen-year-old Rhessa Ann Orr, had come upon a blind construction site which had no required flashing lights and was poorly marked, Orr slammed on the brakes in a futile attempt to avert a mishap. The car skidded off the narrow road and crashed into a tree.

Rear passenger, Pamela Strite, also eighteen, who had managed to crawl out of the wreckage and go for help, Orr, who suffered broken bones and other injuries, and Anspach were all rushed to Harton Medical Center in Tullahoma. Strite was only treated for cuts and bruises. Keith Anspach, after examination by his physician, was transferred to Baptist Hospital in Nashville due the serious nature of his injuries.

For Keith Anspach, the road to recovery had been paved with pain and anguish, but did not lack in grit and resolve. Both on his part and that of his stalwart parents. The accident left him a C4 quadriplegic and confined to a wheelchair. He was handicapped, but not defeated. Far from it.

The families of the victims needed help in dealing with not only the trauma, but the physical and financial difficulties caused by this horrific incident. Believing the construction company had ignored their legal responsibility and contributed to the probability of not only this accident but placed the public at an unreasonable risk, they filed suit to receive just compensation for their losses.

This suit had dragged out in legal red tape for almost three years. Ron had testified in behalf of Keith, who had become a close friend. Keith, ignoring his physical limitations, had enrolled in Motlow, where Ron was also furthering his education in Criminal Justice. This would be only the first leg of a long journey toward success for the ambitious Keith.

Now the construction company had settled out of court.

"Next is the case of the state versus Earl James and Clinton Rivers. Mr. James and Mr. Rivers, how do you plead?"

"Guilty, your honor."

"Clinton Rivers, Earl James, the evidence in this case is overwhelming against you. We have a great many witnesses present today from the law enforcement community who were prepared to testify against you both. You could each have received sentences of up to twelve years on count one, and up to twenty-one years on count two.

"You have chosen to forego a trial and have entered a guilty plea on both counts. I therefore sentence you both to two years on count one and three years on count two, sentences to run concurrent.

"In accordance with agreement with your respective lawyers, you both have been granted thirty days to get your affairs in order. Then, Earl James, you are to report to Hamilton County Jail to begin your sentence. Clinton Rivers, you are to report at that time to the State Penitentiary in Nashville to begin serving your sentence. If either of you fails to report, you have by so doing, revoked our agreement in your respective case, and will face the consequences."

The judge banged the gavel sharply on his bench. "Next case, please."

Ron's heart sank. Early on, Earl James had offered information against former Governor Ray Blanton. Apparently this information was worth more to the legal system than a stiff sentence on these felons.

But life must go on. And so must Ron's pursuit of justice.

CHAPTER NINETEEN

Ron returned to Lynchburg somewhat depressed and furious. The justice system, as he saw it, had undeniably let him down. At least for the next thirty days he would have to watch his every move. Even when he went to church, he would go one route and return by another.

Late one spring evening soon afterward, as dark was falling; the ringing of the phone at his desk startled him from his edgy thoughts.

"Sheriff," the somber voice on the phone squeaked, "there's a fight on the causeway at Lost Creek. We need you right away!"

Ron shook himself and sighed. It had been a long day. As he started his cruiser and pulled on his headlights, his concerns mounted. *Is this for real or just a ploy to get me out in the country after dark?*

He headed up Tanyard Hill toward Lost Creek. Succinctly Steve's words coming in on the radio broke into his emotional silence.

"Sheriff, the caller is back on the phone. He wants to know which way you are coming."

"Of course he does," Ron snapped. "Tell him I'm coming through Hickory Hill and Bakertown."

Hanging the radio mike back in place, Ron immediately changed directions, darting out Campbell Lane toward Harry Hill Road, leading him to Ridgeville Road, then turning right on Lost Creek just above the causeway.

As he cautiously crept toward the causeway, he could plainly see that not a soul was there. The call, as he suspected, had been an obtrusive ploy. As he reached the stop sign at Beech

Hill Rd, the dispatcher again radioed. The mystery man was again on the phone demanding the location of the sheriff. Ron related his findings at the causeway. He then told Steve to inform the caller that he was en route back to the jail.

"He wants to know which way you're coming."

"Tell him you don't know."

Ron turned left and drove out Beech Hill Road into Franklin County and returned to Lynchburg via Highway 50 near Tim's Ford Dam from the direction of Fayetteville.

On April 30th, Rivers petitioned to have his sentence probated. The petition was denied.

Ron stayed alert during the entire thirty days and never traveled the same way twice. Knowing that there were others out there involved in the conspiracy against him who had never been apprehended, he knew that he must plan every move he made with great precision.

Even after the thirty days had expired and Rivers and James had reported to serve their time, other incidents transpired during Ron's tenure as sheriff which removed any trace of uncertainty that the others involved were still not satisfied, and wanted him taken out of the picture.

James petitioned for a probate sentence on several occasions: October, 1980, March 1981, and May 1981. When this proved futile, he repeatedly filed to serve the remainder of his sentence in the State Pen.

Ron made several trips to Chattanooga to block the transfer. Finally, time ran out. The move was out of his hands.

Ron felt that because of his prior connections in Nashville that this relocation could end in a possible granting of the prior requests for a commuted sentence. Because of this, a deal was reached through his attorney, McCord, for early release after two years served with a long probation period of twenty-one years. Ron knew that had he been released through the Nashville Court, the probation period would have been much shorter.

Through the grapevine, Rivers learned of Ron's deal with James and requested an audience with him for the purpose of attempting to arrange a similar agreement.

Ron met with Rivers and his attorney at the State Pen. Ron would agree to grant Rivers' request only on one condition: he must turn state's evidence against the others who Ron knew were involved in the plot against his life. Rivers' fear of retribution from the uncaptured co-conspirators was greater than his desire to have his sentence shortened.

Against his lawyer's advise, Rivers repeated several times, "It's not over!"

But for Ron, his efforts in River's case were definitely over.

During 1982, while serving the remainder of his second term as sheriff, Ron was approached by several persons inquiring, "If you ever are elected sheriff again, will you ever turn your head to criminal activity going on in Moore County?"

His answer was always an immediate and emphatic, "Absolutely not!"

Ron did not win the election to a third term, but still received a substantial number of votes. During the next two years he worked various security jobs, and on Monday, 17 August 1984, was hired by the City of Tullahoma Police Department, where he has continued his "pursuit of justice" and now serves as Captain of Investigation.

EPILOGUE

When Keith Anspach enrolled at Motlow Community College in 1978, his mother, Roberta, attended every class with him, taking notes, and aiding him in every conceivable way. He received his Associate degree in 1980 with a striking 4.0 grade average.

Next it was on to Middle Tennessee State University in Murfreesboro, where he graduated in 1982, summa cum laude, again achieving a 4.0 GPA, and a BS in Computer Science. Then, in 1984 he received his master's degree in Computer Science from the University of Tennessee Space Institute.

"I couldn't have done this without my parents," Keith told me. "They have always been my greatest supporters."

After earning his master's, Keith worked as a sub-contractor for AEDC (Arnold Engineering and Development Center) near Tullahoma for about a year and a half. In 1986, he went to work there as a full time programmer / analyst, and his mother was hired as his assistant.

In the early 1990's Keith took a sixteen-month leave of absence from AEDC, and then continued to work while completing his Ph.D. in engineering science in his spare time. This was accomplished in 1994, after which he was upgraded to the position of engineer scientist.

Because of the unrelenting determination of Keith Anspach and his parents, he even continued his prior interest in art, and with a mouth stick, drew pictures which were used to produce an illustrated calendar each year until 2007.

To Ron, Keith has become one of his personal heroes, and he has continued their friendship throughout the years. He greets each day with a smile, and is truly an inspiration to all with whom he comes in contact.

Since Ron has been serving with the Tullahoma Police Department there have also been many challenging cases. One in particular which comes to mind for him made headlines in the Tullahoma News on Friday August 14th, 1992.

We shall call the man James Lincoln. The headline read, "Lincoln goes to jail after rape conviction".

Lincoln had pleaded guilty to five counts of aggravated rape, nine counts of rape and two counts of sexual exploitation of a minor—a total of sixteen counts, all involving his minor daughter.

This activity had been going on over a prolonged period. A number of complaints had been made to the Department of Children's Services. Each time that he had been in danger of investigation, he relocated with his children, packing all of his belongings in a trailer. Reports also included many violent actions. His wife had disappeared and never returned.

After a number of complaints with no results, the Chief of Police and Captain asked Ron to investigate. Ron sat down with the DCS and arranged to coordinate their efforts on this baffling case. They began by contacting the father of a known friend of the abused girl who worked at the local Castner Knott Department store where the Captain also worked part time. The friend's father gave permission to talk with his daughter, who disclosed pertinent information on the case.

Afterward, Ron, with the DCS officer, picked up the abused girl at school for confirmation. After interviewing her, she was taken to the hospital and examined. The information disclosed by the daughter went beyond anything expected and was extremely graphic and damning against her father. That same day, teachers, doctors and other professionals were interviewed in an attempt to obtain probable cause for a warrant against the abuser. After doing so, Ron went to the Judicial Commissioner, got the warrant, and Lincoln was arrested. Highest possible bond was set, which they knew he would not be able to make, and the abuser was taken to jail. The girl and her brother were immediately taken into custody by DCS. Now Ron would be able to slow down a bit in gathering sufficient evidence against Lincoln to clinch a conviction.

During this time Ron asked questions regarding the location of the trailer. The father, it turned out, had taken it to a junkyard and hid it. When Ron went to the junkyard, he informed the proprietor that he was an accessory to a crime. The trailer mysteriously soon appeared at the Police Department, where it was locked up as abandoned property. Ron then obtained a search warrant to examine the contents of the trailer. When this was done, it was proven that it belonged to James Lincoln. Among the contents pornographic pictures and slides were discovered which further enhanced the case against the suspect.

On the first court date at General Sessions the judge felt that there was enough probable cause to bind the case over to the next Grand Jury.

During that term of the Grand Jury, sufficient probable cause was established, a true bill was obtained, a capias warrant was issued and the abuser was served at the Coffee County Jail. A trial date was then set. In this process his lawyer and the district attorney's office reached an agreement on a plea bargain.

According to the Tullahoma News article, Assistant District Attorney Ken Shelton stated that the sentence of 35 years was the maximum sentence ever imposed in Coffee County for that type of crime.

Coffee County District Attorney Mickey Layne told the Tullahoma News that the arrest and conviction of Lincoln would not have been possible without the work of Tullahoma police investigator Ron Cunningham and the Tullahoma Police Department.

The article further states that Layne singled out Cunningham for praise.

It goes on to say: "'As investigating officer he spearheaded the investigation,' Layne said. 'We want to congratulate Officer Cunningham and the Tullahoma Police Department for their outstanding work.'"

The painstaking investigation had gone on for nearly four months prior to the conviction. Lincoln remains incarcerated at this writing.

It is work like this which helped to elevate Ron to the status of Captain of Investigation where he remains in his quest for pursuit of justice.

PICTORAL

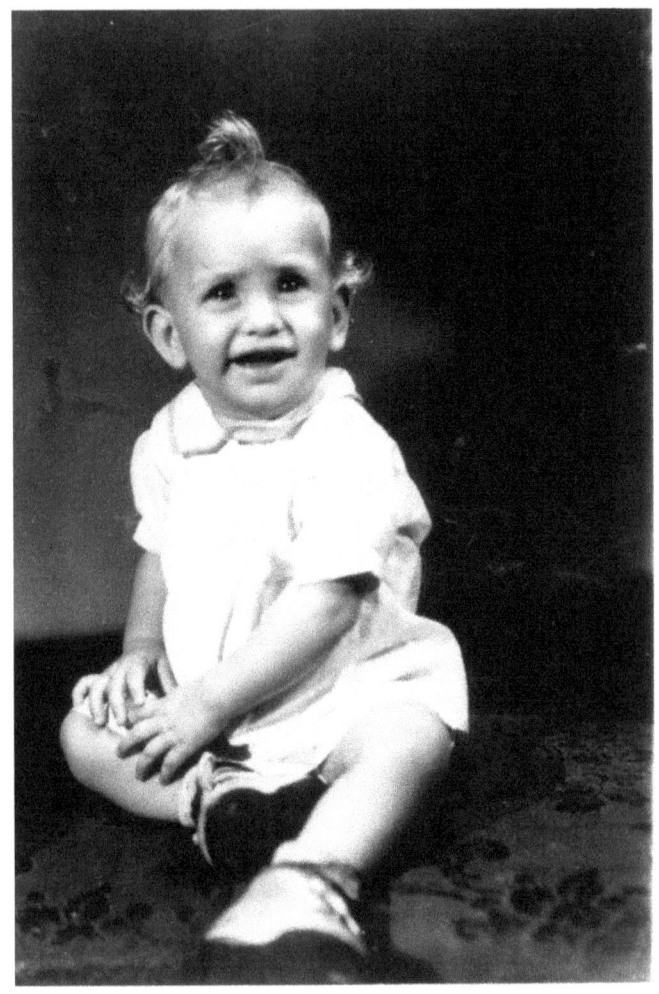

Ron as a baby

Photo property of Ron Cunningham

Recent photo of Ron

Photo property of Ron Cunningham

Old Moore County Jail

Photo Rhonda St. Clair

Post at entrance to Jack Daniel's Visitor Center

Photo Stan St. Clair

Sign at entrance to Jack Daniel's

Visitor Center

Photo Stan St. Clair

Sign at Redd's Grocery

Photo Stan St. Clair

Car in which Keith Anspach was a passenger

Keith Anspach

Panning for gold at Moon's

Photo property of Ron Cunningham

Elvis Wade

Linda Cunningham on a recent trip to Japan

Photo property of Ron Cunningham

Old home place of Richard Cunningham, ancestor of Ron Cunningham, in Warren County, Tennessee

Photo property of Ron Cunningham

Joseph Colonel Cunningham

Pioneer and Confederate Soldier

Information gleaned and rephrased from accounts found in the book *In Deadly Ernest -The First Missouri Confederate Brigade*

By Phil Gottschalk, Missouri River Press, 1991

Coupled with Internet Sources

Joseph Colonel Cunningham was born to Richard and Mary Bickle Cunningham on April 16th, 1835 in Coffee County, Tennessee. He was the fifth child born of eleven, and the fourth of six boys. He had five sisters, only one of which was older than he. He was reared there. Just across the pasture stands the cabin built by his father between 1825 and 1830. Joseph married Mary E. Nichols on December 8th, 1854. Their first son, George Jackson

Cunningham, was born on October 12th, in Coffee County.

Joseph is similar to the present day Cunningham family in that part of his life. Whether driven by hard times, or just by the excitement of adventure, he loaded up his wife and his two year old son, along with their possessions into a wagon and headed to Missouri. They may have had a pair of horses, the wagon and what they could carry in it, along with supplies for their journey. The Cunningham family today is scattered across the country, driven by the same spirit which drove Joseph and his young family across the plains to Missouri.

In 1859 Joseph and Mary gave birth to another son, which was named for him. Now with their four-year-old son, George Jackson, and newborn Joseph, they settled in Moore Township, Oregon County, Missouri. There, Joseph received a land grant of two parcels of property:

one forty-acre tract, and another eighty-acre tract. They owned a total of one hundred and twenty acres on which to farm and raise livestock, hunt and scratch out a living. For the time being, they had their dream. Joseph had to be a very hard worker; a very loyal and devoted type of individual. He was a man of his word. If he promised you something, you could count on him keeping that promise.

At the onset of the Civil War the people of Missouri wanted to remain neutral and not take part in the war. However, the people of the state divided in whose part to take. Early in 1861, a man named Sterling Price formed a state Militia known as the "Missouri State Guard". Its original purpose was to protect the citizens against invasion. Price had sent word to the Union army that as long as they didn't send in any troops, there would be no violence. But some of the Federal officers viewed him as a threat, and moved in troops from Indiana and Illinois, fearing that Price had a ready-made army just waiting to be recruited for the Confederates. The Union army then placed Missouri under martial law and began confiscating livestock, grain and horses for their troops. In some cases the Kansas "Jay Hawkers" who were traveling with the Union army burned entire towns in Missouri, taking the bed covers beforehand.

As a result of the blatant action of the Federals, Missouri was forced to succeed from the Union. In late 1861, Sterling Price sent a message to Jefferson Davis, asking him to accept his Missouri Guard into Confederate service as a part of their army, as they were merely volunteers, and were not being paid. As a result the Guard became known as the First Missouri Confederate Brigade.

These actions are what set Joseph on fire against the Federals and instigated his enlistment with the Confederates. On 5 March, 1862, he voluntarily joined in the fight against the Union's intrusion.

Most of these men had already fought at Wilson's Creek and Lexington, Missouri in 1861, and were devoted to Sterling Price, whom they affectionately called, "Old Pap". Price earned a commission as Major General in the Confederate army on 6 March 1862, the very next day following Joseph Cunningham's enlistment, and led his soldiers across the Mississippi River to reinforce the Confederate forces at Corinth Mississippi.

Cunningham had been assigned to the 4th Missouri Infantry, Company B under Colonel McFarland, General Price's Command.

According to Phil Gottschalk's book, Major John Tyler, Jr. of Prices staff wrote to Senator William Yancey ten days later a graphic description of his eyewitness of the battle in Corinth.

"Redoubts and rifle pits increasingly burst intermingled sheets of flame until the air under its agonizing load of shot and Minnie ball hissed like a serpent. Regiment vied with regiment in braving the fierce terrors in which the earth trembled and the sun appeared to reel. Martin was killed and horses were shot from under Green and Colbert, but still the columns firmly advanced. At 12 o'clock a wild shout of triumph indicated that the entrenchments were carried. The enemy up to this moment had bravely defended them, but he now precipitatively fled, leaving his numerous dead, a portion of his artillery and many captives in our possession.

"Davie's soldiers were so astounded by the impetuous charge of Price's veterans that they retreated several hundred yards to a new position. A Missourian in his charge wrote: 'They ran like hens running from a hawk, hiding behind every log and in every place that they could find. They left several pieces of cannon...We followed them for a quarter mile, but they outran us; we having marched for the last two weeks and marched 10 miles that morning, several of our men gave out."

Quite a vivid description of a harsh and determined band of soldiers hell bent on winning over a belligerent enemy whom they considered unwanted invaders. Obviously Tyler was a very well-educated man for his day.

Another great example of fighting in which Joseph took part was in the Battle of Atlanta, when the Missouri First and Fourth Brigades replaced the Tennessee Regiment during the night after a skirmish in which nothing major had developed. In this battle, General Johnson was searching for the best location to attack General Sherman's army and take out the largest number of men.

The next morning the Federals taunted the Missouri soldiers, expecting little response. Being the experienced marksmen that they were, the Missourians quickly sent Sherman's troops scurrying for cover. The reporting Union soldier described the attack against the defensive Missourians as "grabbing a hornet's nest by the business end."

In December of 1862 President Jefferson Davis paid a visit to the First Missouri Brigade in Vicksburg, Mississippi. There he inspected the troops before going to Granada on Christmas Eve. A Missouri officer described their review like this: "The First Missouri Brigade were clothed in their new uniforms of gray striped with blue, and presented a fine appearance that won the heart of the Chief Magistrate and wreathed General Price's broad face with sunny smiles. Every regiment greeted the former with a Missouri yell—a cross between an Indian war whoop and a Yankee Huzza—to which the quiet intellectual, pale-faced broad-foreheaded chieftain (Davis) replied by facing the colors and bowing low with uncovered head, and with undisguised satisfaction and pleasure."

Davis was very familiar with these troops, as their exploits were widely acclaimed.

Joseph was a man of grit. Many times during his military service to his country he could have gone home to his family, but he didn't. Many others did, especially when things were going so badly for the South. But he didn't. He served every day, marched every mile, at times with no shoes, his feet bleeding with every step he made forward. He couldn't quit! This is where the character of a man shines. This is a good reason to believe that he was truly a remarkable man.

In July of 1864, while serving under Captain Nicks, Joseph was wounded and hospitalized in Meridian, Mississippi, from which he was paroled at the close of the war. He had contracted chronic erysipelas in his left leg, which crippled him in his left hip and knee for the remainder of his life.

He returned to Coffee County, Tennessee, where he passed away in 1917.

BIBLIOGRAPHY

Picture of Ron Cunningham with book, *Conspiracy in the Town that Town Forgot*

The Sunday News, October 4, 2009, Tullahoma, Tennessee, used by permission

Information regarding death of Deputy Charles J. Crabtree

The Tullahoma News, Tullahoma, Tennessee

Information regarding the death of Spring Hill Officer, Corp. Jeremy McLaren

Spring Hill Police Dept.
199 Town Center Pky.
Spring Hill, Tennessee, 37174

Information on death of Corp. Kerry Hayworth

Tullahoma Police Dept.
201 W. Grundy St.
Tullahoma, Tennessee 37388

Photo of Sheriff Ron Cunningham returning to Lynchburg after the FBI sting in which his death was faked

The Nashville Tennessean, February 16, 1979

Official court records from Hamilton County, Tennessee regarding the case against the accused conspirators on the life of Sheriff Ron Cunningham, 1979-1980

Larry Wallace Picture

http://www.tbi.state.tn.us/about_us/former_directors.shtml

Picture of car in which Keith Anspach was a passenger

The Tullahoma News, Tullahoma, Tennessee 8-24-1977

Elvis Wade photo, 1987

http://www.onlineseats.com/elvis-wade-tickets/index.asp

Keith Anspach picture and info supplied by Keith, and some is rephrased from articles from the Tullahoma News, Keith Anspach, an inspiration to all," November 11, 2004

Quotes and some information on First Missouri Confederate Brigade
Joseph Cunningham

In Deadly Ernest -The First Missouri Confederate Brigade by Phil Gottschalk, Missouri River Press, 1991

Some information on Joseph Cunningham was from:

http://www.militaryhistoryonline.com/genealogy/ancestorcomments.aspx?id=1212&state=Missouri&type=4&rid=2339

Definition and spelling of erysipelas:

http://www.answers.com/topic/erysipelas

www.ingramcontent.com/pod-product-compliance
Lightning Source LLC
Chambersburg PA
CBHW062203080426
42734CB00010B/1766